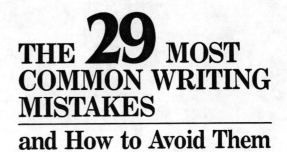

THE **29** MOST COMMON WRITING MISTAKES

and How to Avoid Them

THE **29** MOST COMMON WRITING MISTAKES

and How to Avoid Them

by Judy Delton

Writer's
Digest
Books

Cincinnati, Ohio

Second printing 1986

Library of Congress Cataloging in Publication Data

Delton, Judy.
    The twenty-nine most common writing mistakes and how to avoid them.
    Includes index.
    1. Authorship. I. Title.
PN147.D43   1985   808'.02   84-27117
ISBN 0-89879-172-3

For Jane Resh Thomas, author, critic, friend, and commiserator in this, our delirious profession of scribery.

Contents

Introduction

Not only diamonds are forever. Kirk Polking, of *Writer's Digest*, has said, "Friends and lovers come and go. Your writing is forever."

I find that very comforting. Writing is something warm and dependable to snuggle up to when everything else is in flux. It's a little secret that you carry with you in public—the knowledge that you alone have the ability to escape to a wonderland where you can make anything happen. How many people can do that? By some coincidence, the novel I have just completed has that as a theme. They say novels about writers don't sell, but that was a long time ago, before almost everyone wanted to be one. And why not? It's something you can be without great investment, without a college degree, a license, an attaché case, or a new wardrobe.

Why, then, do so many writers fail? Why are only 5 percent of the writers in America self-supporting? Why does that 5 percent earn an average yearly salary of $4,500? I think it's because they keep making the same incredibly common mistakes. I have been teaching writing and also lecturing around the country for more than ten years, and I read a great many manuscripts, both fiction and nonfiction. On top of these, writers mail me manuscripts to critique. And invariably, undoubtedly, and without fail, the same problems occur. Over and over, writers do the same things that keep them from creating a good story, from selling, and from being one of those 5 percent who are Professional Writers.

Part of the problem is that many writers believe in arrival without leaving home. They believe in talent but not skill. I read somewhere that in no other profession (except perhaps art) is immediate arrival expected. A pianist expects to put in long hours of practice before he plays in concert. A dancer begins training at the age of four or five. And a bricklayer expects to serve an apprenticeship. But for some reason, when a beginning writer puts words on paper, those words are sacrosanct.

And because these writers are enamored of their own words, they don't let themselves discover the criteria for real communication, or what the pitfalls might be that they've fallen into over and over again. John Ciardi has said, "The reason for putting something on paper is to change it." If you are not willing to give up some of your words for new ones (or at least rearrange them), you may not communicate. And your story may be read only by you and your friends and relations.

It is easy to write when you don't know how to write. When I started in 1971 I knew absolutely nothing about it and found it a joy. Sometimes I long for those days—the days I didn't know an infinitive from an infant or a metaphor from a melody. I typed my heart out on that newsprint paper on a card table in my living room, my small son running matchbox cars around my feet. I laughed and cried over my words and read them aloud to anyone who would listen.

The day I found out I was not a perfect writer, the heavens toppled on my head. But the drive to sell my words and support my four children with my writing overcame my pride, and I began to stop generalizing and to be more universal than personal. Kind editors who saw a glimmer of talent pointed out problems, and over the years (and mostly by evolution) my writing tightened up and grew stronger. I began to use verbs instead of adjectives. But never again did I enjoy writing quite as much as I had when I did not know a thing about it.

But there is a time that is almost as fine. That is when your writing talent and skills merge. Then at last you can be as spontaneous as when you began, because good writing will no longer depend on mood—it will have become a habit. It is a gratifying time. I shortened it to a sort of formula:

$$J = T + S, \text{ Joy equals Talent plus Skill.}$$

The writing mistakes that follow apply to fiction and nonfiction, poetry, books, novels, essays, and articles. Some apply more to one than another, but all forms of writing will prosper by their avoidance.

The pitfalls apply to both writing and selling. (Selling your writing means that you have communicated.) Many of the corrections overlap. For example, using specific images instead of generalizing, and communicating instead of self-expressing are part of saying something universal.

There are no clear-cut frames around mistakes. In order to make things as clear as possible, I have separated the headings and let things flow as they may. The fact that some are longer than others does not deem them more important. Some simply lend themselves to my own experience better than others.

You may ask (and rightly so), "Why do you think you know so much about what I should do?" I don't. I only know how I succeeded. I can tell you what I experienced, how I learned what the pitfalls were, and how I climbed out of them. I have published forty hardcover children's books and novels, and 160 magazine articles and stories (and a little bit of poetry) in ten years. I know that sounds like a lot. But perhaps it will motivate you to avoid the mistakes. The pitfalls, after all, are the things I know most about in my life (I know a little bit about fixing lawnmowers, but not as much as I do about pitfalls.)

Over the years, after classes, students have said to me, "Why don't you write all this stuff down?" So that's what I am doing. I am writing this "stuff" down, in the hope that you can profit from it. I will point out the problems and show you how to avoid them. Here's hoping that when you've finished the book and avoided the mistakes, I'll see your byline in print. Cheers!

THE **29** MOST COMMON WRITING MISTAKES

and How to Avoid Them

1

Don't Procrastinate!

When I am at any kind of gathering where I meet new people, or when I am mingling at a dinner party after one of my lectures, at least one of the people I meet inevitably says, "Oh, I could write too, *if only I had the time*—maybe someday after my daughter starts school, or my son gets married, or my . . . " Here her voice trails off into more apologies, enough to keep her from writing for a lifetime.

Others say, "I have an aunt who writes—she is really good too, but she never got anything published because she had more important things to do—she ran for councilwoman in the third district . . . " Or (the most common), "Someday I'm gonna write a book. Why, the things I could write about—I keep them in this little notebook, and someday I'm gonna . . ."

Someday I'm Gonna. Someday I'm going to title one of my books with that very phrase! All of those well-meaning "someday I'm gonna" people somehow never do get around to writing that book, because they are procrastinators. I don't know why more people procrastinate about writing than anything else, but they seem to. Perhaps because it would be so much fun to have written a book but so hard to actually *do* it.

Other people manage to get started but they never finish. After a few lines (or pages) they tear up their work and begin something entirely different. Or they jump from idea to idea without completing any of them.

Another reason why people procrastinate about writing may be that they have never really made a commitment. They have never chosen writing as a priority in their life. They sit down to write something and are blown away by the first wind that sweeps through the room—an appliance needs repair, dinner has to be cooked, the grass needs cutting, the dog has to go to the vet for a shot. All these things are priorities to many of the writers I know. Families are high on the priority list.

It's difficult, or maybe impossible, to have two major priorities. It's like going into a candy store with one quarter—you have to choose! I don't believe this means you have to entirely give up, say, your family. There are many things you do every day that would never be missed if you gave them up. Say you are a housewife. Maybe being president of the PTA could be second to writing. (You could write during the meeting time.) Maybe you could expect more of your children, of your husband or wife. Or maybe some of the things you do would not have to be done at all!

Once I had chosen my priorities, it was clear sailing. I gave up the cooking, cleaning, mending, and gardening that I had done with such zest. I channeled all of that effort into my writing. Till then I had picked and frozen strawberries, canned vegetables, and waited on my children. I decided it was time for a change. I remember the day I told the kids I was going to write for the rest of my life and earn enough money to support us (instead of going to work in a bank, as my mother had suggested). I told them they would have to keep house. And they have, ever since. They've also learned to cook, ever since the day I took the frozen chicken out of the freezer and handed it to my twelve-year-old daughter (herself a published book author now).

She said, "What do I do with it?"

I said, "You have to cook it."

She said, "It is too hard."

I said, "It won't be if you wait awhile or run water over it."

That was the end of my procrastination and the beginning of my writing career. I set up the card table in the living room and acted as a hub (but not a worker) in the traffic around me. I was still at home. I knew what was going on. But my main occupation was now a writer. All the effort I had put into the PTA and cooking and cleaning now went on paper. As I write this I look up and smile. My seventeen-year-old son (who was four when I began writing) is shaking rugs and vacuuming. It was a quiet change in 1974, but it took.

Even if changing priorities is for the best, you have to be *ready* to do it—like dieting—at the evolutionary point in your life where it is important enough to you. And of course you run the risk of it never being the right time if you wait too long.

If you have an office job, you may have to get up earlier to write. If you jog, you may have to type instead. If you bowl after work, you may need to use that time to write. The Saturdays at the golf course, or washing windows, or walking dogs—are they priorities? Dirty windows don't bother me. If they did, I'd work harder writing to earn enough to have someone come in and wash them.

Sometimes people do choose writing as a priority, but even then find it hard to stay at the typewriter. They may actually look for distractions to keep them procrastinating—sharpening pencils, cleaning out drawers, sorting paper clips. Sometimes this is temporary and sometimes it turns into a *bona fide* writer's block.

Waiting for inspiration is like waiting for friends. If you sit around the house and don't go out and meet them, they will never come. You have to make things happen. Writing is an active occupation, not a passive one. It may be easier when you feel "inspired," but you won't be inspired if you don't begin in the first place. Inspiration often comes while you are working, not always in advance. Give inspiration a chance.

Setting a time at your desk and disciplining yourself to write is not as painful as it sounds. Give yourself lots of leeway. Maybe just stipulate that you sit there. Or just type what comes to your mind, playfully. Avoid the attitude that you have to write something Important. If you begin typing something (or writing in longhand if you'd rather), something *will* happen. I have gone up to two months without writing anything new. I've done my editorial mail, my revisions, and my rewriting, however, and that keeps me warmed up. When I do begin something new, I go to it day and night, keep at it until it is done.

Everyone works a different way, but it is important to give yourself a chance to find *your* way, by setting the time each day for something to happen. You want to be there when it does. Here, right up front, are some exercises to get you going, because if you don't *start* writing, none of the other pitfalls will matter!

Warm-up Exercises for the Procrastinator

In sports, players do warm-up exercises to get going. Runners stretch and boxers spar and gymnasts do pushups. Over the years I have accumulated a lot of warm-up exercises for writers. These warm-up exercises not only got writers going, but many times evolved into marketable essays and articles in their own right. Some are more effective than others. Some probe your feelings more deeply and some trigger emotion and lead to meaty, salable work ahead. But if they do nothing else but get you going, get you out of the "someday I'm gonna" rut, and break the procrastination cycle, they will have served you well.

   1. Try this. Close your eyes and think back to your childhood. Think of one special time—one specific incident—one day or moment (not a whole summer), and re-create the feeling in your mind that you felt that day. Write it. Let us feel it, hear it, taste it, see it. Use your senses to let us experience it. Was it an ice-cream cone on a hot summer day? Chocolate maybe? How did it feel melting and running down your arm? Was it a walk across a cornfield in the fall, the stalks brittle and broken? How did they sound under your feet? What did you have on? Write one sentence, or one page, or even more. These warm-ups are open-ended, and there is no way you can do them "wrong," as long as you are writing.

   2. Say something brand new about Christmas, or Easter, or any holiday. Remember: anything; just don't write something you have seen or heard before. Make it your *own* holiday story. Then put it away in a drawer or file for a few days, take it out, and turn it into a marketable essay or story. Magazines need seasonal things and are always looking for something that has not been done.

   3. Open a magazine and read the first line of any story or article. Write it on your paper. Now pretend it is the first line of *your* story. What would you do with it? What would be your second line? See if you can finish it, your way. Do the same thing with the *last* line of an article or story. How would you get to that point? What would have preceded it?

   Now try the first line of a famous poem: "I think that I shall never see . . ." Finish the poem yourself. What would yours be like? Let yourself be wild, silly, bizarre, sad, wistful, sentimental, serious. "O Helen, thy beauty is to me . . ." What would your next lines be? They would *not* be "Like those Nicean barks of yore that gently o'er the perfumed sea the weary, wayworn wanderer bore to his own native shore," because you are you, and not Edgar Allan Poe. It is your own rendition, no matter how frivolous, that you want to try.

4. Write about everything in life you don't like, (or do like)— but you must do it in only thirty words or less! It will require good thinking and tight writing, and the use of just the right words. Do not be general. Be very specific.

5. Go to your medicine cabinet, or spice rack, and without looking at the names on any of the bottles, open the caps and slowly, one at a time, with your eyes closed, take a sniff. Sniff each one, taking your time to savor it, until you come to one that triggers a memory. One of them will be a signal to write. Write what you remember, *without identifying the smell*. Don't worry about structure, about punctuation, about form. Just get that feeling down on paper. When I have done this exercise in class, *vanilla* is the scent that gets most of the class writing. It is the "Grandma's kitchen on a cold winter day" feeling. All sorts of feelings go with smells. Sage could take you back in time to Thanksgivings on the farm, or rubbing alcohol to a bruised knee. Or it may be a different smell entirely that will be your memory trigger.

If you don't have spices readily available, try perfumes or powders or even garage smells like gasoline and oil. Be aware of smells and let them lead down roads to other times and places.

6. Open up your purse, attaché case, desk or bureau drawer and see which item triggers your imagination. Write about any one of them, but just one (a ticket stub, bobby pin, credit card, lipstick, coin, etc.).

7. Open a book, and the first word that your eye falls on, write about it. If the first does not trigger anything imaginative, try a second. A dictionary is a good book for this. Point your finger to a word (more specific than using just the eye), and when you come to a word that moves you, write about it.

8. Write about an object as if it were alive. This is an "I" exercise; in other words, you have to *be* the object. Examples: be an earring, a clock, a box of candy, a shoe, a car, a lightbulb, a pencil, or anything else that is not alive. You give it life! Get inside of the thing and write from its perspective.

9. Write about a relative of yours—any relative, one you love or one you hate, or an imaginary one—a nonsense story about an imaginary person.

10. This is an exercise to get you writing in which you need a partner. Ask your husband, wife, son, daughter, friend, or co-worker to do it with you. It is similar to role playing. Tell the other person to be a taxi driver and you be a fare who has only a fifty-dollar bill. He can't change it. You just talk. Pretend. See what happens. Do this orally and then when you are well into it, *stop, and sit down and write the dialogue* you just had.

You can also pretend you are a shopper accused of shoplifting; a parent with a son who does not want to take piano lessons; the mother of a daughter who wants to stay out overnight; an IRS auditor and a taxpayer whose deductions are questionable; or a waiter and a dissatisfied customer. The possibilities are endless.

11. These are my favorite block-breakers—*titles* and *first lines*. I very often use them in classes, and every time I do, one of the students sells his warm-up exercise! Try it and see if you do. I will list titles. Pick one (or try them all), put it at the top of your paper, and let it be a trigger for whatever you want to write. You have the title; all you need is the story to go with it. You may write one sentence and quit, you may write a page, or you may finish an entire story on the subject. Or it may become a nonfiction article.

With the first lines, instead of putting one at the top of your paper as a heading, you simply begin your story with that line, and keep going. If there is a blank, just fill it in and keep going. If just one of these does not get you out of your procrastination, you will perhaps need to do one of them each day—or one a week. No matter what the schedule is, if you give yourself the assignment it will be one leg out of the nonwriting rut! Here they are:

TITLES:

My Grandma Grew Roses (This could trigger memories of your own grandma, and real or metaphorical roses. No two people who write this story have similar results.)

Seven Paper Men (Paper dolls? Lumber mill? Weaklings? *Your* paper men!)

Just One Small Blade (Razor blade? Blade of grass? What is *your* blade?)

Licorice Sticks and Icicle Picks

A Clean Sweep

Tape It

Ten for Your Money

I Hate All of Them (Or you can change it to *I Love All of Them*. Feel free to change titles and use or discard as *you* need to.)

Too Far Away from Here
Wire, Mire, Boats for Hire

FIRST LINES:

It's not my fault that _____.

If I were you for just one day, I would _____.

If I had been born one hundred years ago, I would

_____.

No one told me that _____.

It is all my mother's fault that I _____.

That was the summer we went to _____.

Mine is a lot more _____.

The morning it happened, it was _____.

I am expecting a _____.

Marge and Harry began to _____.

She sat by the door listening for the _____.

I am not taking the blame for _____.

The doll was made out of _____.

2 Don't Talk Away Your Story or Article Before, or Instead of, Writing It.

It is fun to talk about ideas, so much fun that it becomes a favorite pastime of writers when they meet. "I've got this great idea for a novel!" Author A says to Author B. "Just listen to this—it's all about this girl who wants to commit suicide and it's set in Alaska and she's got this cousin from . . . ." They order more coffee and before long, hours have gone by, hours when some of the story could have been written. But now it may never be written at all because the author (A) has got it out of her system and seen reaction and praise and has no real need to actually write it.

It is probably because this talking away is so common that Lawrence Block says, "Don't hire Carnegie Hall for the third Saturday in October if you like to sing in the bathtub." Having an idea (or a bathtub song) is not the same as having a written book (or an opera). As they say, talk is cheap. But in this case it may be costly.

7

I once had a very good writer-friend. She had ideas, she made me think, she generated stories, and we spent many hours every day "talking writing." I believed that she was the best thing that ever happened to me. She helped me find stories in things I would never have seen without her help. I didn't know (and still don't know) many writers who do that. I worried that someday we'd part, for whatever reason, and what would I do? How would I get along without this person to brainstorm with? There was no doubt that the friendship and talk was a good thing, and that it made us grow as writers. But when she actually did move away, I would never have believed the result.

My lack of communication with an idea person, a writer, must have driven me to the typewriter. (I did not realize at the time how little I had been producing, what few hours I spent at the typewriter, and how many hours we sat in restaurants, talking.) When she left, I must have communicated with my typewriter and worked out my ideas on paper, because since I have not been with her, talking my life away, I have produced six books, three of them in a new genre, and I have not suffered from the writer's block that I knew frequently in those past years.

So fight that urge to tell everyone your marvelous idea, at least until your first draft is on paper. Write your story—don't talk it away!

3 Don't Try to Write the Best Story or Article in the World. Don't Be Afraid to Fail.

Compared to other occupations, writing is cheap. Since the Second World War has been over, America has had paper, so you need not hang on to the sheet that you roll into your typewriter as if it were your last. In the art world, I can understand the Fear of Starting. My daughter is an artist and some of her paper costs five dollars a sheet. I would be afraid to put a brush mark on that, too.

In my beginning writing classes, the first thing I do is give my students permission to write badly. I say, "Do not sit down in front of the typewriter with great expectations. Sit down ready to simply play, to talk on paper. This is no time for strict criteria. This is time for honesty, exposure, and the freedom to say whatever you want to say—fiction or nonfiction, spelled or misspelled."

Tell yourself no one has to read this, that you can throw it away, or you can hide it in your underwear drawer. And you can. No one even need know you wrote anything. When you have no expectations, you cannot fail. What might happen instead is that you could love what you wrote, and want to read it aloud just to hear the sound of your own words. Even if you don't love it, you have nothing to lose. If it isn't perfect but is worth saving, you can always rewrite it. The main thing to remember is that it is not engraved in concrete or steel or even indelible ink.

Use newsprint to begin with. Looking at that cheap paper will convince you that this is just a game—a game you could win at, but you don't mind losing the first round, either. Better yet, handwrite your first efforts. This does not look so official, and may be less intimidating than the typewriter. Remember, there is an eraser, there is a wastebasket, and everything you write does not have to be God's truth or the great American novel.

Many years ago I taught a class called "Fear of Writing" (probably in honor of the title *Fear of Flying*—Jong had just published it). Housewives and students and career people flocked to that class, intrigued by the title, and all had one thing in common: they were afraid to write. Each harbored a secret wish to be a published writer, but none of them could live up to their expectations of what a writer should do. They suffered from a form of worship of the written word, a sort of perfectionist complex. Even picking up a pencil in that class caused panic to set in.

The first thing I did, when they stopped shaking, was to tell them to write down what they had eaten for breakfast. There were surprised looks. "But that isn't writing," exclaimed one woman.

"Of course it is," I replied. "It is definitely writing."

They all went eagerly to work. They had no idea writing was this easy. They went from listing bacon and eggs to telling how things tasted, and even the ones who only had coffee wanted to say why. I couldn't stop them, once they started. After ten minutes one woman raised her hand and asked if she could go on and write what she'd had for lunch! Another woman wanted to tell me on paper about her dinner party last week, and another, a new restaurant near her house.

Try that if your expectations for yourself are too great. There are always breakfast, lunch, and dinner to write about.

The following day in class I told the students to write about what they would do with a million dollars if they found it, and where they went on vacation last year. When they got the idea that this indeed was writing, this indeed was telling a story, they moved on to what they really wanted to say. Everyone needs permission to be less than perfect.

I read somewhere that a student went to a teacher saying, "I have lots of ideas and experiences but I don't know how to begin. I'm afraid to start." The teacher said, "Pretend that on the way home from work you passed a burning building. Flames were leaping out all over and huge fire trucks were pulling up to the scene. News reporters arrived. What would you do when you got home? You would probably tell the nearest person all about it. You'd say, 'Guess what happened to me on the way home from work? I saw flames leaping out of the windows of that old warehouse on Tenth Street, and before I knew it the whole block was ablaze.' "

"Write like you talk" isn't just a cliché. People who can tell a story with great enthusiasm seem to think *writing* it is different, that they don't need that enthusiasm and zest in the typewriter. They do. You must go to the typewriter and write the story just as you would tell it to a neighbor or your wife. Oh, there will be some loose ends. There will be the Ohs and Ahs and semicolons that can be taken out later. In fact, whole sentences may be taken out later. But for now your job is to get the story down as you would orally. Write like you talk? Absolutely—at least in the first draft.

Another reason writers have trouble getting started (and it is tied in with perfectionism) is that they have so much to say. Beginning writers I have met tend to want to say everything in one book, or one article. At my summer writing camp last year one camper had enough material in her story to expand into *five* stories! "Choose one," I told her.

It is very important, when you start, to set limits. Too much freedom is always inhibiting. Once, at the university where I was a visiting lecturer, I had to wait in the hall for a previous class to vacate our classroom. I struck up a conversation with a writer and asked her what her previous day's assignment had been. She said words I never will forget: "Oh, we don't have any special

10

subject to write about. Here at the university we have total freedom. We can write about anything we want to." Here she paused and frowned. And then she said the Memorable Words: "I find all that freedom inhibiting." At that minute I changed my lecture plan and spoke instead on too much freedom. It *is* inhibiting.

Everyone needs limits. If I say in a class, "Write about bubble gum," or "ink," or "your vacation," the whole class is writing in a moment. But if I say, "Write about anything in the world you want to," they sit and look stumped. It *is* inhibiting. So set some limits for yourself, something not too big, and give yourself permission to fail. Then you will be able to put a brush mark on your paper.

4 Don't Wear Blinders. See Life Through the Eyes of a Writer.

Two people can walk down a street together—even sit in a room together—and look at the same things but see something different. That is why it is so important to look at life around you. You must *listen* and *see* to be a writer, not in Africa or Bermuda or lands of excitement, but right here around you, going and coming from work. I give my students, as a first assignment, the order to eavesdrop on a bus or in a restaurant and write down conversations word-for-word. What people say indicates character, in fiction or nonfiction.

Often conversation is a power play, with one speaker more aggressive than the other. For example, one man may be boastful. For every accomplishment his friend tells, he tells one of his own to surpass it. Or perhaps you will overhear the conversation of a whiner, a person who has a worse lot than anyone. Her bills are bigger, and illnesses graver, and days shorter than those of her friends. These people are your *cast of characters*.

There is a very successful filmmaker whose specialty is commercials, and he has won many awards by being an eavesdropper. He watches, he listens, then uses the ordinary man in the restaurant, bus, or Laundromat in his films. While other commercials preach and are boring, his are sophisticated and humorous and have artistic merit. Clara, the original "Where's the beef?" lady, was one of the characters he found by listening to the man and woman on the street. He finds *real* people, which is what you have to do to write strong prose. Your eavesdropping may not turn into a story on the spot, but it will be stored in your mind for a time when it will appear in your writing. The main thing about eavesdropping is that it gets you looking at life, at real people.

Writers look and listen, and they see and hear relationships. They know that overheard conversation on a bus can turn up in a picture book. The awareness that such relationships exist means ideas for your books and articles. The eavesdropping you do provides a key to personality and character; an hour at the Laundromat may pay off in your notebook. Writers need to learn to listen.

A friend and I sit on the beach at the lake. My son is painting the house. He says it looks like rain. I say, "Rain before seven, clear before eleven." As I say it, my friend smiles and lights a cigarette. She hears only a platitude, an old proverb. I hear instead something that I could make into a picture book. A boy procrastinates, watches for rain so he can stop painting. He would have other procrastinations, of course; list three, and I have a picture book. Or I could write about a rain forest, or about clichés and proverbs. Or I could write a nonfiction article on weather, the myths and how they began. I take out a notebook and jot these things down. My friend has by now forgotten the proverb altogether. She can afford to. She is not a writer.

If you are a writer, you cannot afford to look at life with blinders on. You can't just light another cigarette and change the subject. Everything people say and do is grist for your mill and ideas for your notebook. My friend and I go indoors, turn on TV, and watch reruns of the old sitcoms. She and I both see *Bob Newhart* and *Mary Tyler Moore*, but while she is laughing and forgetting, I am turning them into animals for a fantasy. TV shows are marvelous triggers for animal characters. Can't you picture an animal who is always counseling his friends—an amateur psychologist-type? Or an animal that works in a news room? There are endless possibilities, free "triggers" to get your mind spinning and your fingers typing. Friends who don't see what you see are not slow—they simply are not writers.

When I visit schools, teachers often ask me, "How can we get the children to write?" I always tell them that first you have to get them to think. And to think, they need to look and listen. You don't teach "creativity"—you teach awareness. If they become aware, they may think. And if they think, they may write.

In *Backyard Angel* (Houghton Mifflin 1983) I began with only what I saw—my daughter on our back steps, sulking. A friend of mine walked around her on the steps and said, "A nickel for a smile." That's all I had, what I saw. So I rolled this character into my typewriter to see what she would do. The rest was discovery. I "discovered" that she had a younger brother named Rags and that she was in charge of his life, and that her mother worked and that in the end she was less lonely and was even able to smile because she met a friend named Edna.

Discovery happens when you give your unconscious mind a chance to use all that information gleaned in eavesdropping, and in experiencing life. You trust your unconscious "bank" of experience, and you let it come out.

The idea for *My Mom Hates Me in January* (Whitman 1975) was just a title. I was working on an article at my typewriter and my small son (small at that time) kept asking questions. Impatiently I said, "Go away, I'm working," and "Let me alone." His response was, "Boy, you're sure crabby in winter."

Now many people (nonwriters) could hear this and smile; or hear it and ignore it; or hear it and feel guilty. But a writer thinks, *With some changes, that would be a good title for a picture book*—a picture book about a mother who is waiting for spring. Spring would, in fact, be the solution to the problem! A writer sees relationships between "Boy, you're sure crabby in winter," and a book called, more appropriately, *My Mom Hates Me in January*. I stopped the article I was working on and wrote that instead. I let one word follow another and discovered that the crabby mother was not the little boy's fault at all. It was simply that winter was too long.

Be aware of possibilities. Always ask yourself, "What if . . . ?" One evening I watched a television special on aging, and it showed some senior citizens going into homes with small children and becoming foster grandparents. I imagined us doing that. As I thought, my mind began to spin with the experiences my son could have with a foster grandfather (his is deceased). I saw birthdays, fishing trips, evenings by the fire listening to stories of the past. I thought, If we took a foster grandparent in, I could write a book about it! I'd call it, *The Artificial Grandpa*.

In the middle of the night I awoke with the thought that I need not actually experience this—I already had created it in my mind. I quickly wrote it just as it *could* have happened. In fact, it *had* happened. I didn't have to wait a year for the experience.

It has been said that writers are fortunate because they get to live their lives twice: once in the doing, and once in the telling. If a writer finds consolation escaping to his childhood and examining it and getting inside of the child he used to be, he experiences this twofold existence. It means that, as well as looking at the life around you now, you look at the life you used to live, too.

The *Kitty* books are about myself, growing up Catholic in the forties. Until I began that series, my only experience had been writing and publishing picture books and magazine articles and poetry. My mind spun with episodes from my Catholic school days, and since *Roots* had just been published and minorities were becoming very popular in children's books, I thought, Now is the time. (Timing is important in publishing.) So I sat down and gave myself permission to write a bad book. I kept typing, and remembered to defer judgment. I used things that happened to me as the chapters, and when I ran out of my own experiences, I borrowed from my daughter's life and my friends' lives.

I really had cut giant paper dolls out of old cartons with a friend during the war, and I really did lock myself in the bathroom because I couldn't find "do" (as in "do re mi") in music class. Little things, but real things. And when we lived in Wisconsin, my daughter and her friend really did go uninvited to weddings and receptions of strangers at the Catholic church. It was something that Kitty would have done. My characters were myself and two friends—one religious and righteous, the other fun-loving and liberal-minded. Neither one was as extreme as the characters in the book. I exaggerated their personalities as well as my own.

I also draw on my past for my picture books. In *Two Good Friends* (Crown 1974), American Library Association *Notable*, the duck is my mother. Animals in a fantasy story are not animals and the story is not an animal story. It is a people story. The animals have all the characteristics and foibles of very specific persons. Duck is the same kind of perfectionist, the same kind of fanatical housekeeper, that my mother was. My mother swept and cleaned and polished after me, just as Duck polishes furniture and puts paper under Bear's feet when he eats brownies, and watches for falling crumbs. Bear is more of myself, a better cook than housekeeper. The story evolves around the way Duck and Bear exchange their strengths and help each other out. The strength, however, is in the character, above the plot. And the character came to me because I did not wear blinders, but observed and remembered what my mother did and how she acted.

I only had to go back a few years to spot my mother for a character in *Penny Wise Fun Foolish* (Crown 1976). She became the ostrich who collected coupons for money-off of items in stores. I used to take my coupon-collecting mother grocery shopping and there was always a bit of confusion at the check-out counter while she tried to find the right coupon for the right store. One day I thought to myself, my mother could be an animal who collects coupons.

There is, by the way, no significance in the fact that my mother is portrayed as a duck, or an ostrich. Any animal is suitable; using an animal instead of a person simply gives an author more freedom. One can do funnier things with animals, crazy, bizarre things that might be offensive if one used real people. A fussy person-housekeeper is not funny, but a fussy duck is. During a school visit a principal asked me to look at the children and tell him what animals they reminded me of. I made sure he understood that people do not remind me of animals. The animal is simply a vehicle used to portray human characteristics.

Characterization in fantasy is not quite as simple as I've portrayed it—an author needs something to happen, and a plot with a problem, and the problem needs a resolution, but I got the main thing, the character, from just keeping my eyes and ears open.

If you write nonfiction and need ideas instead of characters, material is still out there in plain view, waiting for you to take off your blinders and see it. The newspaper, for example, has a wealth of information. That basketball score of Saturday's wheelchair teams can lead to an in-depth article on the players, their personalities, their hobbies, their aspirations. Or it can lead to a fictionalized story of what could happen to a member of the team.

Last night's old movie on T.V. could pique your interest in the "old stars." Whatever happened to Betty Hutton and Sonja Henie? Are they still alive? If so, what are they doing today?

Consider the ad in tonight's paper for a winter coat that you love, but it costs $350. Does your city have a thrift store where you could get that same look for $20? Ideas require not only clear vision of everything around you, but the ability to relate what you see, to twist and turn things to fit a story.

Sometimes a friend tells you a story that is just too good to pass up. With a little imagination, it could become a story or article. How often have you said, "I should write that down." It is a good thing to trust your unconscious, hoping that ideas will return when they are needed, but it also does not hurt to give the memory some help. Write down those things people say. Turn them into something on a rainy day.

People you work with every day are especially good grist for your mill. The continuity of your relationship can provide not only character for your writing, but theme and plot. What has happened over the years in the place where you work? What is universal about it? (That is, what will people relate to?)

Some of the office people, just like some of your collected conversations at the bus stop, restaurants, and Laundromats, can directly trigger an article or story. But most of the material needs to be collected in your mind, and on paper (in a sort of idea file), to incubate. I learned to trust that file, trust the incubating ideas in my unconscious mind, and sure enough, they did turn up in my writing when I gave them a chance. The lady on the bus, the man in the diner—there they are on paper, four years later!

So don't close your eyes—to the past, or to the present. An idea isn't a book, but it is the thing you need to begin.

---

5 Don't Edit As you Write. Don't Stop to Admire—or Chastise—Your Work.

Sometimes I watch writers work. Many of them (the ones who can't meet deadlines and the ones who say, "It takes me so *long* to write a story or article") type a sentence, stop, and go back and read it. Then they judge it. "Is it good or bad?" they say to themselves. "Does it belong here, or in the next chapter?" It is a common habit and a great temptation to read your work over, line by line. But it is *fatal*.

Do not edit as you write. Do not judge as you write. Do not change what you just wrote. Don't correct the spelling of the word you just wrote. That's a lot of *don'ts*, but the writer who rewrites as he goes will never finish his piece. Give yourself a chance to get better, to unwind on paper, to expand, to flow freely. In fiction I write to discover, and if I stopped after every word or phrase I wouldn't have the chance to discover anything.

Even if the piece *is* good, you can't see it when you are so close to the material. A writer needs distance and a body of work to judge effectively. In the end you may toss out all of what you have written. In my last novel, at the last minute I discarded the whole first chapter, part of the second, and opened the book with the more active episode in chapter three. Would I have had that chance to see it as a whole if I'd edited each line? Put completed work in the freezer for a period: a day, a night, even a week or two. Then read it and make the changes you think it needs—but only when it is cold, not hot out of your typewriter.

When I read my work through right after I have written it, I do one of two things: I love it passionately and believe I am a genius or I hate it passionately and believe I have lost my talent, skill, marbles, or all three. Probably neither one is valid. If I read it a week later, I have clearer, cleaner judgment. I read it as an outsider would. I put myself in an editor's mind and read it with her perspective. If I don't like it, I find some way to remedy it. Rewriting will be covered in Mistake 21, but for now just let yourself *write*. Editing comes later.

6
Don't Generalize. Use Specific Images.

Avoid abstractions; be concrete.

Last summer at the university where I teach, a man read a story about his vacation. He hop-scotched over the tops of many experiences: camping, swimming, barbecuing, fishing. I stopped him as he gave only one line to a marshmallow roast.

I said, "You have a swimming story, a fishing story, and a camping story. Choose one. Instead of glossing over the marshmallow roast, tell me about it. What did it feel like? Look like? Taste like? Let us feel the evening, the fire, the friends. Let us see the stars, the fire-lit faces. Let us hear the songs, the sizzle of the fire. Is it midsummer? Fall? Spring?"

Let us see the wart on the nose of the miller, Chaucer's famous character. The miller differs from everyone else because of that wart. The wart is specific. There are lots of men with brown hair or blue eyes, lots that are tall or short or of medium height, but there are not many who have a wart on their nose with hair growing out of it. It is a writer's job always to look for warts. A wart gives us imagery. Brown hair does not. A crispy, light brown marshmallow, hard on the outside and soft and sticky on the inside, gives us imagery. A "roasted marshmallow" does not.

Develop the habit of being specific. For example, instead of talking about a "board game," use its name, e.g., "a game of *Risk*." Instead of a pink dress, call it mauve. Instead of saying the smell was "bad," say very specifically what bad smell it was, as "It smelled like sour milk."

An editor will spot generalities, or abstractions, that have no image. She will watch for things that get right down to the very specific. If she is looking for an article on building a picnic table, she won't buy the one that says, "Buy some wood and nails and pound them with a hammer." She would more likely opt for one that says, "Get Norway pine and saw it into six lengths six feet long, six inches wide, etc." and "Buy half-inch screws, etc." (This example may not be accurate, but it is specific!)

When you went to the dentist, how afraid were you? What did the dentist wear? Could you see the hairs in his nose as he bent over the chair? What else could you see from the dental chair? Read Nabokov's description of having a tooth extracted! "A tongue like a seal exploring vast empty caverns."

Someone once said, "Never write about mankind. Write about a man." A man called Henry, with a scar he got in Vietnam and a love for Chinese eggrolls. Henry is specific—man is general.

General is: The house was big and old. It stood on a lovely hill. Specific is: The farmhouse had a crack in the bedroom that looked like a rabbit's face. The paper was peeling off the kitchen wall like old dried scotch tape and if you were not careful when you went downstairs, you'd trip on the step with the board missing.

Sinclair Lewis is considered a very minor novelist by some. They say he never made it to the great stage, although there is a museum on Main Street in his honor. His characters do have lots of contrived dialogue stuck in their mouths to get across the author's personal messages. Long and windy, Red Lewis waxes didactic. But there is one thing that makes his books classics, makes them absolutely memorable. It is his imagery—his very specific images. It makes his writing readable because you can *feel* the restaurant on Main Street with the sticky oilcloth on its tables.

"Axel Egg's General Store was frequented by Scandinavian farmers. In the shallow dark window space heaps of sleezy sateens, canvas shoes designed for women with bulging ankles, steel and red glass buttons on cards with broken edges, a graniteware frying pan reposing on a sun-faded crepe blouse."

About Billy's Lunch Counter: "Thick handleless cups on the wet oilcloth-covered counter. An odor of onions and the smoke of hot lard. In the doorway a young man audibly sucking a toothpick. An aluminum ashtray labeled, 'Greetings from Gopher Prairie.' "

There is no doubt that Red Lewis *saw* things in his hometown. As he grew up, whatever else he did, he observed, and when he grew up he made use of everything that was stored in his mind. If you close your eyes you can go back to that place with him and experience what he did, so accurate is his reporting.

As with anything else, specific must be used in moderation. Don't overdo a good thing and pile details on top of details, ending up with a boring description that people will want to skip over. The specific images must contribute to the point you want to make. When reading the story over "cold" (in the editing process), put yourself in the reader's place. Are these details going to bore him? Are there just enough to make the point, or are there so many that he loses the point? Specific images are almost always better than generalizations, but don't go to the opposite extreme in your zest for perfection.

7 Don't Tell, Show. Use Dialogue and Incident, Not Long Narrative.

Do you remember, as a child (or maybe even last night!), reading a book, all curled up comfortably with an apple perhaps, or a box of candy and a fire in the fireplace, and then you came to a long passage of description and you felt a bit bored? Your eye (you found) was slipping down the page, just grazing the words, moving along, skipping words, skipping whole sentences, searching for something. What was your eye searching for? It was looking for something to *happen*. It was looking for *action*!

Most long narrative is boring. What is narrative? Narrative is telling a story, instead of showing a story, endless pages where nothing happens but description. *Mary said she was going to the circus* is a narrative phrase, a *telling* phrase. *Mary said, "I am going to the circus!"* is an *action* phrase.

Don't fall into the mistake of *telling* too much. Try to *show* everything that happens. There are three ways to do that.

1. Dialogue (conversation)
2. Incident (a happening)
3. Anecdote (a story about a happening)

Another way to keep the *telling* mode is to keep everything in the present tense and the active voice. If you write passively, it tends to bore. (Passive is: "The clothes were washed by the girl." Active is: "The girl washed the clothes." Passive has a "helping" verb.)

Dialogue is the best way to break up long narrative. When individuals can say something themselves, in fiction or nonfiction, let them say it. If you interview people for an article, don't tell what they said, but let them say it themselves. Use quotes when you have a chance. Put the words into their mouths. When a reader sees quotation marks, he is enlivened. He may not even realize it, but he is. He reads on. And a writer needs every device he can find to keep that reader reading. Look over the last piece of writing you did; see how many quotation marks you used.

Incident is another good way to break up long narrative. An incident is having something *happen*. Movies and plays and television sitcoms are based on this. It would be no good watching a movie unless something happened. And it's no good reading if something doesn't happen—an earthquake, a walk around the block, a car chase, a cooking class, an explosion, sibling rivalry, a party. Dialogue is good, but the characters can't talk the whole time. Something has to *happen*.

Speakers (and writers) who hold your attention use anecdotes. They say "I met a man on the way to the studio . . . ." An anecdote is the telling of a story within a story. The Bible uses this device in the parables. So follow the example of what is said by some to be the world's greatest book, and tell a story to break up the narrative.

Some authors use narrative very effectively. They manage to hold the reader's attention and keep his eye from wandering and his fingers from turning pages, just by *telling*, even when it is at some length. But it is the author's style that allows this. He may have a strong narrative style, a special talent with his telling that makes it absorbing. Most writers need something more. I get manuscripts every day that say, "This is a picture book," and if they didn't tell me I wouldn't know, judging by the *telling* instead of *showing*. In writing for children, telling instead of showing is disastrous. Children's books are not easier to write because they are shorter. (A student once told me she wrote poetry because it was easier, since it was shorter!) It is just the reverse. In a children's book or a poem there is no room for error. Picture books are *action*—every word counts. Given a three- or four-year-old child's attention span, lots has to happen very quickly. There is no room or time for description. The picture does that. Your job is to move the words along that page rapidly and fluently and with lots of incident, anecdote, and dialogue.

In my writing classes I have the students print in their notebooks in very large letters, SHOW, DON'T TELL—SHOW, DON'T TELL—SHOW, DON'T TELL—three times for emphasis. E.B. White said that Professor Strunk used to grab his coat lapels in class and say, "OMIT NEEDLESS WORDS. OMIT NEEDLESS WORDS. OMIT NEEDLESS WORDS." Everything three times, and I am sure it did no harm to his writing students in 1920. Neither does SHOW, DON'T TELL. And if you have not read the "little book" of Strunk and White called *The Elements of Style,* be sure you do. Like the dictionary, it is one you can't afford to be without.

8 Don't Forget to Contrast and Compare.

The secret to being original lies in the ability to see relationships. If you describe something green, for example, and grass has already been used, think of something green in your life that is like the thing you want to describe.

Things can be either *like* something (simile) or they can *be* something, symbolically (metaphor). Metaphors and similes are most effective when they are natural and spontaneous and plausible. When writers strain too hard to find a fresh image, the result can be pretentious, or ludicrous. Here are some effective similes:

We zigzagged about the country like a bluebottle in a jam jar. Similes always use "like" or "as" in the comparison.

The customers were folded over their coffee cups like ferns. (Steinbeck) Isn't that a clear image? A furled frond seems to have just the character needed here to portray a row of coffee drinkers at a lunch counter, perhaps tired from a morning's work. The curved fronds and the curved spines come together just right to create an image! Notice the originality in that short comparison. Are your comparisons that strong? They can be; there are "ferns" in your life, too. You have to look for them and use them.

The dog inspected me, and wagged his tail as a professor wags a pencil. (Steinbeck) How does a professor wag a pencil? I'd say slowly, for emphasis. The dog's tail was just as slow, out of caution.

His face was lean and shriveled, like an apple too long in the barrel. Have you seen apples too long in the barrel? I have seen one too long in the hydrator pan in the refrigerator, back in the corner. And it is shriveled, like a prune, almost. If there has been a shriveled apple in your life, you could have made this comparison.

Here are some strong metaphors:

He was completely round, a perambulating carbuncle of a man. (T.H. White) I love this picture, and I have seen this man. A moving boil, all pink and soft, I'm sure!

The man who read the commercial message for foot-ease shoes had marshmallows instead of tonsils. (E.B. White) Close your eyes and listen! That soft, mushy voice—as soft as the foot-ease shoes.

The school bus, seeing us waiting at the curb, swept to a halt, opened its mouth, sucked the boy in, and sprang away with an angry growl. (E.B. White) Here is a personified school bus, and a fine metaphor. You may have seen a bus suck people in and growl away, but have you ever used it to make a comparison on paper? That is what makes the difference between successful writers and ones who keep wishing.

When you read, keep track of what other writers use to compare. For one of the best examples of contrast and comparison ever written, read Ray Bradbury's short story, "The Sound of Summer Running." He takes an ordinary pair of tennis shoes and puts marshmallows into the soles, and the sinews of deer, and other fresh new meanings that transport the reader right along with the boy in the story, a boy who simply gets a new pair of tennis shoes. You will never look at a pair of tennis shoes the same way again, and you will never again be satisfied with ordinary comparisons.

Don't say things the way others do. Contrast and compare with original things from your own life, and see how your writing stands erect and takes on new life!

Don't Depend on Adjectives. Use Strong Verbs.

There was a time when strong writing depended on adjectives. Or at least adjectives were very popular. And many beginning writers (and some "ending" writers) still believe that the strength of effective writing is in lining up modifier after modifier in front of a noun, that the more pretty, descriptive words, the better. Actually the exact opposite is true. Adjectives weaken; the fewer you use in an article or story, the better.

If you are describing a man and say, "The tall, dark, handsome, virile young man. . ." we don't know much more about him than we did before you described him. It is better to choose one strong adjective that is more specific than several weak, general ones. Try "the dapper young man" or compare him to someone everyone knows. And it is even better to use no adjectives at all. Save your strength for verbs. The strength of all good prose (and even poetry!) is in verbs.

I give my students an assignment of picking up any book or newspaper and looking for strong verbs. Most students are not even aware of verbs before the assignment. Try this yourself. It will increase your awareness of what makes good prose, and it will help you to be a more critical reader. Chances are that some of your favorite pieces are favorites because of the verbs.

"Collecting" strong verbs can be done only in context. One cannot "list" them. Their strength is relative to the context of the sentence. The reason the verb needs its sentence context is that a strong verb is not just a big word; a strong verb is a common word used in an uncommon place.

In the sentence: "The woman sat thinking about how to get revenge on her husband," "thinking" is the verb. In this case it is not a strong verb. It is weak and ordinary, something in the category of walk, run, talk, say, etc. What the sentence needs is not a bigger word than "thinking" but rather one that is not usually associated with revenge. For example, "The woman sat embroidering revenge." Do you see how the sentence comes alive and takes on new strength? Because "embroidering" is a word that we usually associate with sewing, the minute we remove it from the stitching environment and place it with revenge, it becomes a strong verb. It also works because it is womanly, intricate, time-consuming, and fits the situation. Not every verb would do—the image must be suitable.

If you use the word *rake* to say the man raked the grass, it is common. Take *raked* out of that sentence and put it in another one, for example: "The man's eyes raked her body," and it takes on immediate new significance. *Rake* is now a strong verb.

Hunt for strong verbs in context. In your verb hunt, be careful that those chosen are not: 1) clichés, or 2) contrived. Don't reach too far for a verb and come up with something outlandish. An overdose could lead to Purple Prose, where the writing is so strung with big words, excessive metaphors, and lengthy description that the very communication is lost.

Saying "The desk spawned paper" is stronger than saying "The desk was messy." "Barked the butcher" is stronger than "Said the butcher." But saying, "She excavated the contents of her handbag" is pedantic, and describing a person as "a fellow toiler in the factory of life" is indeed purple prose. Sincerity disappears in these far-fetched attempts, and their banality stands out instead. Sometimes less is more, and "lawn" can be more effective than "verdant sward"!

So file those adjectives and value those verbs. Put them to work for you.

10 Don't Use Clichés, Qualifiers, Platitudes, and Overdone Words.

Anything worth saying is worth being original about. It has been said that there are no new ideas under the sun. That may be, but there are new ways of seeing and saying things. There are new relationships. New comparisons. You learn by imitation. Walking and talking are imitative, and when you begin to write, you write things that are much like those you've read. But as you evolve as a writer, you must find your own voice.

It is astoundingly easy to slip into cliché-ridden writing. I can "date" a new writer, tell him how long he has been writing by how many clichés he uses. My old essays are full of clichés. Looking through my scrapbooks from the seventies one night, with my son-in-law looking over my shoulder, I was embarrassed at the number of clichés, platitudes, and overused words.

If you want to describe something white, don't say it was as white as snow. Choose something, anything, in your own experience that was white. White as snow is old and common and it is not yours. Try "white as a freshly laundered sheet"; or "white as a clean sheet of typing paper." Clichés are phrases such as: hard as rock, bright as the sun, thin as a rail, overcome with grief, sick at heart, and thousands more. They are anything someone else said, an arrangement of words not your own. Sometimes a person thinks what he says is original, and it can still be a cliché. It's easy for the typewriter or pen to slip into trite expressions because these phrases are the first thing that come to mind. Be deliberately aware in your reading and writing, and identify and exorcise hackneyed expressions.

Sometimes an editor will call a whole piece of writing a cliché. That means the whole thing has been said—the idea, the form, the theme, the plot. Old hat. Trite, banal, hackneyed.

Editors need fresh new things. I have had students in critique sessions hold on to a yellowed manuscript written ten or twenty years ago, telling me, "But it is about something historical, so it is still good."

Chances are it isn't. It is hard to make a ten-year-old manuscript fresh. Writing about the Civil War in 1916 is different from writing about the Civil War in 1985.

Historical writing takes on the significance of the period in which it is written. Have you ever watched an old movie of George Washington's time, made in 1940? Inevitably, the hairstyles and cut of clothes of 1940 show through, even though the actors wear powdered wigs and brass-buttoned uniforms. George Washington does not appear the same in a movie made in 1940 as he does in one made in 1985. And neither does a manuscript. An old story or article needs more than updating, it needs rewriting.

Along with clichés, it is well to avoid platitudes. Platitudes are trite truisms that are not only commonplace but tend to give writing a banal, didactic, or pompous quality. At one time perhaps they were real "words of wisdom," but today they are overused and outmoded. Some of them are: "It never rains but it pours," "A stitch in time saves nine," "Easy come, easy go," "It takes one to know one," "The calm before the storm," "The early bird gets the worm," and others of the same ilk.

Time has wrought the same destruction with words like wonderful, beautiful, lovely, cute, etc. At one time years ago when a cave man picked a rose and said to his mate, "This is beautiful," it probably had imagery. It said something special about a flower. Today it does not mean anything specific. We don't know any more about the rose than before. Is it red, is it wet, is it closed or open, are there dewdrops on it, does it smell good? Tell me something, anything, about it, but don't tell me it is beautiful.

When you say you met an interesting person, I don't know a thing about him that I didn't know before. Why is he interesting? What makes him interesting? Does he speak nine languages, run in a marathon, have two heads? Does he water ski on his knees, sing Italian opera while juggling thirty pickle jars? *Interesting* is an awful word. It is weak, spineless, and hasn't a jot of imagery.

Avoid qualifiers as well as clichés. A qualifier is something that takes a perfectly clear, decisive statement and weakens it. It is a wishy-washy word that drains strong statements of their validity. Qualifiers are words like just, even, like, although, also, besides, almost, maybe, if, but, too, unless, sort of, etc. Beginning writers use a lot of them. At my writer's camp this past summer, two of the girls told me that if avoiding qualifiers was all they learned (and it wasn't), it would have been worthwhile. They had no idea they used seven qualifiers on a page, and when we took them out and read the sentences without them, they could not believe how much stronger the prose became.

"My brother went along, too." (My brother went along. Period.) "I think maybe I'll have peas. They're as good as beans, almost, anyway." (I'll have peas. They're as good as beans.) These weaklings qualify things so that a writer or speaker never has to take a stand, never has to make a decision. He can eat his cake and have it too, pleasing both sides. A new writer who is afraid of risks (anyway) finds them convenient and satisfying (sort of).

Before we leave clichés and qualifiers, I want to add a related topic that I find in manuscripts even when they are otherwise done professionally: the use of slang, jargon, and idioms in the narrative.

A character in a fiction piece can use slang, jargon, or idioms, if it is in character for the person to do so. But the narrator in fiction or nonfiction must be careful not to slip into the habit. The narrator is an objective reporter who does not call attention to himself by using any dialect or slang. Sometimes a writer may be in a hurry and lapse into street language because he isn't taking the time to censor or polish his narrative. I read a piece recently where an otherwise conservative writer said a character was "in the dog house." She probably meant she was in trouble, but using an idiom to say so is offensive to the reader's ear.

Jargon like "at this point in time" and "I know where you're coming from" is also clichéd and has no place in narrative. Slang like "ain't" and "ya" is more obviously undesirable, and expressions such as "to get ripped off" or "to make out" have no place in narration. All of these follow trends, and besides weakening prose, date stories and articles and render them short-lived.

11 Don't Overdo Punctuation.

Teachers tell me that it is hard enough to get students to *use* punctuation; they surely don't ever want to tell them *not to*! That must be one of life's cycles: working hard as a child to learn the myriad symbols that define our language, and then growing up to find you use too much. I did.

In 1972 I had just begun to write nonfiction articles for magazines. I loved exclamation points! I used to use several!!! Even many!!!!!!!!!!! When, to my dismay, the editor of the magazine for whom I was writing an assignment piece on farm auctions told me, "Judy, keep these to a minimum!!!!!!!!! In fact, you may not need them at all."

Not need them at all! Impossible! I was naked without my exclamation points! My sentences were not clothed and they were motionless. I sadly followed his advice. It took me a long while to feel good about giving them up (and I never entirely succeeded) but it made me very aware of how easy it is to depend on punctuation as a crutch for weak writing. You simply will not try to write as well if you pepper your prose with signs. For that is what too much punctuation does. It acts as a signpost to tell the reader how to feel. "Feel excited now!" Or, "This is supposed to be funny! Or startling! Or amazing!"

Beginners tend to use lots of exclamation marks!, semicolons; dashes————. Someone who has been writing for a while for publication is down to the bare minimum. Semicolons can carry a sentence on to infinity; it need never end; just keep on. Periods are necessary. Question marks? are necessary. So are commas,,, and quote marks""""""". But that is really all you need. The rest are crutches that weaken prose—and poetry. Underlining is another thing that some depend on, and CAPITALIZING. (I do it a lot.) It is a way of saying, "Look, this is important. Pay attention. Emphasize this." Whereas, if your writing were adequate, tricks wouldn't be necessary.

I tell students to try to write letters without any !!! or ;;; or ——. They find it very difficult. But whether students succeed in giving up extra punctuation or not, they become aware of what they're doing, and awareness is a good thing. It's one thing to break a rule when you know what it is; it's another to break it when you are not aware that it exists. And sometimes your punctuation can label you a beginner. For a clear and simple guide to the rules of punctuation, read Strunk and White's *The Elements of Style*. It will help you use just enough punctuation, not too much.

Wasn't it Gertrude Stein who wrote a whole book in one sentence, using semicolons? She (supposedly) knew the rules and was taking a poke at all of the writers who did not. Don't be one of them. Make your words do the work instead.

12 Don't Forget Your Theme.

The theme of an article, essay, story, poem, is *why* you are writing it. And it is *what* you are trying to tell us. (Plot is *how* it happens.) A theme is just as important in a picture book for children as it is in a nonfiction article or a novel, or a poem. Steinbeck said that any novelist should be able to state his theme in one sentence. A good title does that without giving away any of the plot or content of the work.

When a student writer begins to read a piece, I ask him or her to tell me the theme in one sentence. That often isn't easy—not to tell the things that happen, not what it is about, but what you want me to know when I am through. The theme is a sort of underground railroad that runs directly through the piece from one end to the other. You can't always see it, but it's there. Stop on those sidetracks and you become distracted. It slows down the trip. It is a digression.

Sometimes a reader believes he is reading about one thing, and on page 4 he finds he isn't reading about that at all. I recently read an article which, on page 1 I believed to be about plant care. (This was an unpublished manuscript, by the way.) I became intrigued because I like plants, but on page 3 the plant motif disappeared cleverly. The writer digressed to speak of a neighbor with a green thumb, and somehow got involved in talking about her dog. "Aha!" I thought. "This is an article about dogs! I was mistaken; it just took a bit to get into it." I like dogs, so I read on, intrigued by the green-thumbed-neighbor's dog, until I came to page 6. On page 6 the dog disappeared, and the article appeared to be about the marital difficulties of the dog/plant owner.

By now I was angry. I'd been misled. I don't like to be misled or tricked when I read. I like honest writing, with an up-front author who puts all his literary cards on the table. Digressions can sometimes be valuable, but not in a case where they are totally misleading. If an article is about plants it should begin with plants, have a middle about plants, and end with plants. All the digressions should enhance the piece, not distract from it. In this article it was anyone's guess what the theme really was.

Because fiction is thought to be a creative medium, writers sometimes think they can be experimental. And they can, but if they want to publish their story, it still needs a theme. The theme is often implicit; it is not directly stated in words. A theme is sometimes the "message" in a story, but this should never be obvious. It should instead be covert, leaving room at the end for the reader to discover the message. Sometimes the reader may even think that he is the only one who knows what the message is, so subtle is an effective theme. No one wants to be preached to, and if the theme is too obvious it will be didactic.

The theme of my new novel, just out with Harcourt Brace, is that the main character is imprisoned by her strict religious upbringing. That is surely also a message. Whether it is preachy or not depends on how it is handled throughout the book. Generally, if incidents are used to show the theme, it will not be as preachy as *telling* would be.

Because the best themes are subtle, the theme of the same book may be interpreted differently by different people, depending on background and experience. Even critics may differ on the theme of a book. I believe the theme of *Of Human Bondage* is that emotions rule the intellect, and that all of us are victims of our heart. Someone else may find a different theme in it.

I think it's obvious that the theme of most of Fitzgerald's work is the decadence of society, but others may disagree. A theme leaves room for interpretation (in fiction), yet it needs to be in the author's mind as he is writing. In a nonfiction piece or book the theme or message can be more overt and less open to interpretation. If an article is called "Skiing Across Country with Your Family," the theme is probably just that. If it is called "How to

Live on a Food Budget with a Family of Five," the theme of the piece is right up front and direct.

Keeping the theme in mind means making an outline of your work either in your head or on paper. You need to have a map and know where you are going or you will end up somewhere you don't want to be. Sometimes it works well to write the end of your story or article first, or at least know how it will end. Keeping your destination in mind will keep you on the right road.

13 Don't Forget: You Need a Beginning, Middle, and End.

That sounds obvious, doesn't it? Yet I see manuscripts every day that lack a beginning, a middle, or an end. Editors surely must see them, too. A piece of writing, fiction or nonfiction, has to be a unit, like a matching wardrobe—color-coordinated. If you start with a red dress and a white hat, and end with green shoes, you are not a unit. Neither is a story or article.

A good many writers lack a beginning, a middle, or an end, because they digress. In a nonfiction article, it is usually a good idea to tell the reader what you are going to say, then say it, and finally say what you have said. An article needs an outline, either on paper or in your head, so that you know where you are going and where you are taking the reader. Tell him that this article is going to be about how to build a bookcase. Then tell him how to build it—what kind of lumber and nails to use, assembly directions, etc. At the end sum it all up, so that we know we are at the end. Some articles trail off. I go paging on in the magazine or newspaper to see where the rest of the article is, and it is nowhere.

Some articles start in the middle, before you are ready. And a good number of them change in midstream, from how to build a bookcase, to some unrelated experience of an uncle's. In both fiction and nonfiction, a beginning is the only chance you have to hook the reader. If you don't capture his attention there you do not have another chance, because he may already have put the magazine down, or taken the book back to the library. Worse yet, the editor may not be hooked, and put the manuscript on the pile destined to be rejected. No matter who the reader is, he has to be caught up in a fresh, vital start.

The way to make the beginning fresh and vital is to open with a bang. Put your best foot forward. Put your best anecdote up front. As I mentioned earlier, in my last novel it was not until the book was almost in galleys that I discovered that the third chapter should really be the first chapter. The third one was where all the description stopped and the real story, and the action, began. Much of the description was not really necessary at all and was discarded, and the rest was woven in with the later story.

Often it is best to write your article or story first (after fashioning an outline) and then eliminate any nonvital part in the beginning that obstructs the reader's vision. Let him see the strongest right away. The strongest will usually be something active, something that plunges you in head-on. Maybe it will be an anecdote. Examples (something very concrete) are very good attention getters. Or you may have someone talking, saying something very rousing, such as the old example, " 'Let go of my leg,' she said to the plumber." The beginning is also an introduction, and may present your premise, or the topic the article is about. Whatever your opener is, you want it to be something the reader can't put down.

The middle is the "meat" of the article, or the body of the story. The plot advances there, the characters unfold. If someone has been hooked on your fine beginning, the middle is the place you can't let them down. The topic or premise will be expanded and explored, and action will occur. You work your way to the climax or main point of the writing.

Endings summarize and give closure. All the loose threads of an article must be tied, and all questions put forth in the piece must be answered. If you write an article on refinishing furniture, be sure that you tell the reader everything you can about it, so that he is not left with a bedstead stripped of its finish, with no directions for applying the stain and sealer.

The end of a piece of fiction should also give the reader some feeling of closure. This is done in many ways. Some authors, like Daphne DuMaurier, go so far as to begin and end a novel with the same sentence. Her *My Cousin Rachel* begins with "They used to hang men at Four Turnings . . . they don't do that anymore." and it ends with the very same line. But the in-depth story between those two lines makes the technique credible and meaningful. It is an effective technique and there is no doubt about the story being a unit.

Pre-typewriter planning can help establish unity. I try to think out an article or story in my mind until it has a good hold. Then I make a simple outline on paper to assist my memory; sometimes it is only a list. Keeping my theme in mind prevents meaningless digression. I often write it down also, and keep it in front of me. Thinking the idea out, mapping out the beginning, middle, and end on paper—all aid in assuring that I have a complete and unified story.

14 Don't Lose Your Balance and Don't Digress.

Many writers skip over important material that you want to know more about, and then slow down on the insignificant parts, dawdling about on street corners when you want to get moving. This gives writing a top-heavy effect—everything in one place, and nothing in another. The article or story is like an hourglass with all the sand in one end.

Put your story on an imaginary scale when you finish. Does it balance? Or is one side much heavier than the other? If it is, put it back in your typewriter and pace it. Take out that paragraph describing the deer in the woods—it won't be missed; expand the part about how he feeds in winter; add a line or two to his habitat. That is pacing. Don't try to say too much in one place.

There is another kind of balance, balance of the sentences. Have you ever read a story aloud (maybe to a child) and tripped over the words? Where the words don't flow, but bunch up and attack? This is because the author is unable to write by ear. He has no sense of music, which is necessary for writing. The lack can be remedied in part by varying the sentence length—some short, some long, and by reading aloud to see how the words *sound*. There should not be a verbal obstacle in every sentence.

A similar problem is changing the subject, or the setting, without warning and without a connecting link. When you move about from one place to another in your article or story, you need transitions. In one of my first picture books, I had two animals engaged in some mischief in a mythical village, and when they had finished it, I said, "Duck opened his door and went into his house." My editor asked (on the manuscript), "How did he get there?" I thought that was a silly question. He must have walked there. But she assured me that you cannot assume anything in writing.

Even if the transition is only one line long, it must be there. It must get a character from the village to his house, from the boat to the shore, or tell how one subject relates to another. I added one line, saying something like "Duck said goodby to Bear and started the long walk home." Then he could validly open the door and go into his house.

Connect your writing with what went before. It is easy to digress while you are writing, and lose track of *where you are*. If you do digress in a piece of writing, it must be for a purpose. You must not digress on a whim about something in the beginning, and then never bring the subject up again in the story. Echoing Anton Chekhov, Edward Albee has said, "You can't hang a gun on the wall in a play and not use it. If there is a gun on the wall in Act I you had better use it by Act III." The same goes for a story, article, or novel. If you hang a "gun" in your story, use it.

15 Don't Self-Express, Communicate.

Self-expression, like soul searching, belongs in a journal. Once, at the lake where I write often during the summer, I had finished a particularly grueling section of my novel. I had dinner that evening with my neighbor, and I expressed relief to be past the emotionally draining section. He said (naturally enough), "What is this book about?"

I replied, "Oh, I guess it is autobiographical. It is about my life—my marriage and divorce and all its tribulations."

I'll always remember his reply. He took a bite of his pork chop, then waved his arm across the table at me, saying, "Save it for the confessional."

It was because he was so close to target that I'll never forget his words. Many of the things I wrote needed exorcising before the book went to press, and to exorcise, you need to put your personal life in the freezer for a while. "Save it for the confessional" is very much like "save it for your journal." Some things are too personal, too general, too maudlin and yes, too boring, to write for publication.

I used to visit high schools and speak at the creative writing classes frequently. The students inevitably brought me small bits of penciled paper, scraps of their heart. There were also completely full spiral notebooks, where their blood was shed on every page among their chemistry notes and math formulas and small sketches of teachers in caricature. It was very, very important to them that I read every word.

I could tell from reading one line what the entire notebook was full of. Feelings. Teenagers feel a lot. And it seems an appropriately fine place and time to write about them.

No one says self-expression is bad, and I am sure psychiatrists and psychologists would say it is very good for you. The mistake comes when the writer thinks all of his feelings are salable, and almost all of them do. I found that each one believed his feelings were unique. I didn't want to tell them that the previous week I had been at another high school in another city or town and read the same things word for word.

What is the matter with self-expression? It is general, it is unoriginal, it is boring, it is trite, and it is sentimental. But mainly it is noncommunicative. It does not seem to be all of those things to the writer, and at some time in everyone's life some things need to be said. But to others, someone else's self-expression drags. Surely it does to editors.

In 1971, when I began to write, I thought my soul searching was extremely original. I had no idea it had all been said. I wrote about Life and Death and Love and sent my soul out in the mail. I was doing all the self-expressing then that I should have done in high school, but I was a generation late. Underneath my verbosity something positive must have showed, because editors took time to tell me that this was not poetry, and that I should read if I wanted to write.

Editors today are busier than they were in the seventies, but if they had time they would tell you the same thing. Read poetry, novels, essays, magazine articles, even advertising. Read critically, and turn your self-expression into communication. This means that your tears over your lost loves, your anger at teachers, the establishment, and parents, and your adoration for a rock star *are* material for writing, but not in that personal, vulnerable form. See how other authors handle those same feelings and gripes (maybe in an editorial essay). Read about how to write objectively and, if necessary, take a writing class to give you information and perspective.

As a writer you must grow beyond your personal feelings into more universal ones. Soul searching is a phase that can be written out. As time passes and your writing evolves, a greater distance, perspective, and objectivity occur. You need not try to rewrite your journals. Those same feelings will show up in your new writing, but in a more original and sophisticated and universal way.

16 Don't Get Personal, Get Universal.

If you read something in a book or magazine and snap your fingers and say, "Boy! I know just what she means! I have felt that very same way," the reason you liked it was because the author was writing something *universal*. It touched a feeling in your life you thought was unique to you. It established a bond between you and the author. But many writers (like many speakers) do the opposite. They go on and on about something that is small and common and lean, that no one cares about.

Does that mean everything you write has to be Deep and Heavy? Or general instead of specific? Or not personal at all? Absolutely not. Some things that are personal are of interest to everyone. Some things that are personal are of interest to no one. Erma Bombeck is universal, which is why she is so popular. Her experiences are unique, but everyone understands them. You say, "That is just the way it is at our house!" and either the situation, or the feeling, *is* the same. One of her lines is, "I am surrounded by women whose pleats never separate when they sit down." No one else had thought of that line. And yet every woman, fat or thin, understands what she is talking about. Unique but universal. Now if she said, "It seems that all the women I meet are thinner than I am," it would be ho hum and boring. It would be common. Many of us have thought that, or said it. But dress it in pleats, and it is uncommon, and very funny.

A good thing to remember (I like to think I coined it myself) is that *only the unique is universal*. That may scare a writer for a moment, thinking it is difficult to locate the unique. It isn't. *Every single thing that has happened to you* is unique. It has not happened to anyone else in exactly the same way. Your experience on a farm on a June day in 1950 will not be exactly like anyone else's experience. But if you tell yours specifically, others will say, "That is just like something that happened to me." Or "I felt that way."

Write about things the reader can get his teeth into. Remember that you know things that no one else in the world knows until you tell them. And when you do tell them those things, they will snap their fingers and say, "I know just what she means—I have felt like that myself!" If you are specific, if you show instead of tell, you have a greater chance of being universal.

17 Don't Preach or Opinionate. Let the Reader Discover for Himself.

Someone said, "If you have a message, call Western Union." Don't write a novel. That is good advice. While I have mentioned in talking about *theme* that it is a message of sorts, it shouldn't be obvious. It should be subtle. This is true with nonfiction and fiction alike, a book or a short story, an essay, or an article. No one likes to read a sermon. Moreover, no one cares about your opinions unless you are President of the United States (and even then they may not care), the recent Nobel prize winner, or a doctor who just found a cure for cancer.

Opinions can find a suitable place in a letter to the editor, or on an Op-Ed page, where magazines solicit opinions. Or you can write to your representative or councilman. You can even print flyers and hand them out if you like causes, or shout your opinion from your open window. But if you are a writer and want to publish, a didactic piece of writing will get you a quick rejection slip.

A preachy article implies that your way is the only way. It is a one-sided argument, and you are hoping for a captive audience—the reader. Even if your piece made it to print, you would lose your reader after he read a few lines. Didacticism also implies that you know more than anyone else on a subject. It wears an air of pompousness—self-righteousness—being holier than thou. Stay away from that and strive to be objective in your writing.

If you list the things wrong with the world, it's like saying, "The world is a terrible place and I am the only good, wise person in it." So don't say things like "Christmas is too commercial." Even if it is true, it is your opinion—one person's opinion. If there is a way to proffer an opinion at all it would be through an incident, an anecdote, or a parable. Give an example of what you want to say, and let the reader discover the opinion for himself.

Art Buchwald once wrote an essay about the commercialism of Christmas that was both humorous and effective. But he never mentioned the word "commercial." His first words in the piece were something like, "Should we close the churches on Christmas? Having them open poses a parking problem, and a threat to free enterprise. Businessmen are angry to lose business and housewife-shoppers are disgruntled." In the end, it is the reader who discovers the message and says in surprise: "Maybe Christmas *is* too commercial."

Have you ever had friends tell you about a wonderful movie? They rave and rave about it and you arrive at the theater with great expectations. After you see it, have you ever been disappointed and concluded, "It isn't *that* good"? The same can be true of a book. This happens often to me. It's called *oversell*. It prevents you from discovering that movie or book for yourself.

The discovery element is extremely important in reading. An author said once, "Readers are getting smarter; they want to put their own egg in the cake mix." Readers want to contribute to the story, to have a part in it, to think. If you tell too much, spell everything out, they feel they aren't being given credit for a brain, they are being talked down to, or patronized. Let the reader do some work by leaving some mystery. If a person knows all about someone and there is no mystery, it is boring. The same with a story. It is boring to know everything. Let the readers participate by letting them put their own egg in. Don't give them every single ingredient; just give them enough to make sure the cake will rise.

If a writer writes something saying, "Abortion is murder," it is preachy. True or not, you lose readers. The reader needs to discover for himself that abortion is murder. How? I read an essay once in which the author spent the time playing on the reader's emotions, involving the reader with the unborn baby. She described the baby's hair, projected to the sunny summer days it would play with its siblings and parents, the report cards it would bring from school. Then the last line in the essay (it was in journal form) said, "Today my mother killed me."

I resent the dishonesty of that approach very much. I don't like to be tricked into reading something. But it is one effective way of projecting an opinion without saying, "Abortion is murder." The reader, who is now emotionally attached to this fictional child, will say it himself. (But it is difficult here to ignore the fact that the reader has been manipulated.)

Related to preachiness is reader implication, also a common mistake of beginning writers. It means that the writer uses the word "I" instead of "I" in his writing, in his conclusion and judgments. If you do this you are implying that the reader thinks exactly the same as you do. When I read something that says *we*, I get very angry, just as I do when I see a dishonest movie or read a dishonest book, because I don't want an author speaking for me. Let him speak for himself only; he is the only person he can be sure shares his opinion.

An example of implication could be, "We must do something about birth control . . . " (or pollution, or overpopulation, or crime.) Not *we*. *I*. If you are the one who believes it needs doing, you can only speak for yourself. The same is true of "It is up to *us*." This is offensive to many readers.

So let the preacher give the sermons at church on Sunday (where people go willingly to be preached to); avoid including the reader in your judgments; and if you have a message, call Western Union!

18 Don't Think of Fiction as False! Honesty Is Essential in All Your Writing.

When I visit schools and speak to children, one of the things I ask them is, "What is fiction and what is nonfiction?" Every hand in the auditorium goes up, and the child I choose will invariably say, "Fiction is something that is made up. It is not true." And then they go on to the reverse of that, "Nonfiction is always true."

I like to redefine the terms on the spot, and tell them that while fiction is a "story," the best fiction is always honest. I go through my own books, which are fresh in their minds during a visit, and point out that Kitty is really me, growing up Catholic in the forties. I may not have done everything she did, but I am Kitty. And Kitty is me. I point out that the duck in *Two Good Friends* is my mother, that she was a clean housekeeper. And that the thing to remember is that all writing must be honest, fiction or nonfiction.

Honesty is not the same as truth. A person can be an honest writer and not always tell the truth. In my novels some of the things are "made up" or exaggerated—the incidents. Perhaps they come out of someone else's life. Maybe a dress I remember was red and I turn it into blue. Maybe the main character was an only child and I give her a brother and a sister. These are simply "facts." They can be played with and turned upside down and rearranged and added and subtracted. Who you are as a writer cannot be manipulated as readily. Your value system, your creed, your culture and background, your emotions, your education, your experiences—none of these can be changed from red to blue with a snap of the fingers.

Effective writing is done from the inside out, not from the outside in. When I was a child and tried to write a story for a class assignment, I was never successful. That was because I was always on the outside, looking at a story as a story. No one ever told me (and I doubt it would have mattered if they had) that writing is more personal than that. I always felt removed from what I was writing in those long-ago situations. I can remember sitting with a sharp pencil and a clean paper, and trying to write a story or essay. I didn't know how to think like a writer, or write like a writer, and I spent all the time trying, instead of taking out of me what was honestly inside. I thought it was something you did, not something you were. Now I know that if I have to try to write well, I am not writing honestly. And dishonest writing is easy to spot.

I spot it in a book I'm reading when I become angry. An anger rises up in me that is at fever pitch by page 21, and I throw the book across the room in a rage. I can't always define immediately what, exactly, is dishonest, but I trust my emotions. Upon exploring further I will find that the author is writing something she does not really believe. It isn't the facts of the story. Those can be carefully garnered. It is writing about growing up Catholic, when she has always been a Protestant. It is the feeling behind the facts that says, "I don't really believe this." An author cannot hide that. You need not always experience something firsthand to write about it, but you must *experience* it, vicariously or emotionally.

John Updike says, "It is my duty as a writer to record life as I know it." That may be the single most important quote in the writing world. It is your own experience (vicarious or real), your beliefs, your attitudes and emotions that you are best at reporting. This is the only way you can report validly. Yours is the only life you can get inside of. It is the only life from which you can write credibly.

It has been said that a writer should "write what he knows." What else could he write? Only dishonest things. A writer can *know* things, however, in many ways. He need not live every experience to report it; he can know many things from research, from reading, from interviews, from a deep interest. If you want to write, and your first choice is to write about the childhood of a person growing up black in Africa, when you really grew up white in Albany, New York, your writing may not be honest. A critic could say, with good reason, "What does she know about being a child in Africa? Who is she to tell me?"

Honesty is probably one way of defining literature. What makes a book a classic? Why do some books last and some turn up at rummage sales for a few years and then disappear altogether? Classics like *Anna Karenina* are usually based on character. And the author is inside of the character, writing from the inside out. Tolstoy *knew* Anna. She was not "made up." Dickens knew Cratchit. E.B. White knew Charlotte. Maugham knew Philip Carey. Fitzgerald knew Diver.

Books (and sometimes movies) that are not based on honest

characterization, but rather plot, may make a big splash but are lost in a few years. Stories like *Jaws* and other plot sensations simply do not stand the test of time. An observer may note that *Jaws* and *Moby Dick* are both stories about fish, but one is so much more—because of honesty, and character.

In more contemporary writing, Anne Tyler has lived with her characters very closely; how otherwise could we live with them so intimately in *Celestial Navigation*, *Earthly Possessions*, and *Dinner at the Homesick Restaurant?* Flannery O'Connor said, "It is better to discover a meaning in what you write than to impose one."

What you write will not lack meaning if the meaning is in *you*. Discovery happens when you are honest. Writing *Kitty in the Summer* I discovered that my grandfather did not like me. I found that he always looked over my head when he spoke to me, never at me. I didn't know that before. And I found out that my aunt Katie liked me better than I thought she did at the time. Honest writing is full of surprises.

If you think you may still have trouble being honest in your writing, try reading a novel you truly like, and at the same time, read the author's letters, or autobiography, or journal. Read *East of Eden* along with Steinbeck's *Journal of a Novel*. Read *The Murder of Roger Ackroyd* and Agatha Christie's autobiography, or her *Come Tell Me How You Live*.

Read Flannery O'Connor's *Habit of Being* along with her stories "A Good Man Is Hard to Find," or "The Lame Shall Enter First." You will never wonder where the misfit came from, or little Mary Fortune, after you read how Flannery lived in the farmhouse (Andalusia) in the deep south with her mother, Regina, their peacocks and peahens and peachicks, and the earthy hired help that lived in. Her illness and confinement and her isolation contributed to her making good, honest use of life from her bedroom window, and she wrote about what she knew and loved. And it was a violent rendition. Her mother's friends used to ask, "Why doesn't Flannery ever write anything nice, about good people?" I could tell them. It was because she wrote about what she knew best. And not all of what she knew was nice and good and nonviolent. She chose to report life as she saw it, which is why she wrote lasting material.

To write honestly is to take risks. If you are not ready to take risks, you are not ready to write for publication. If you play safe and say, "I can't write about my life while my mother is still alive," or "I can't write that gothic while I have small children," you may never write. To write with great restraint is to write dishonestly. To write effectively, a writer must be ready to spill a certain amount of blood on the sidewalk. Poets and novelists, I suppose, more than nonfiction writers, stand naked in front of strangers. Are you ready for that kind of exposure? Are you ready for the consequences and ramifications of the writing life? Every day I get manuscripts in the mail to critique in which the writer did not spill a drop of blood; he did not expose himself; he didn't take any chances. Because of this, his manuscript is totally unoriginal and clichéd with cardboard people traversing his plastic landscape. It will never sell.

Besides exposing your own blood and guts, you may expose other people—friends, enemies, neighbors, relatives. The risk complicates. For the most part, people do not recognize themselves in print and there can be enough changes in the "facts" to put them off. Not everyone has to stick with his whole life as closely as Thomas Wolfe did in *Look Homeward, Angel*. Sinclair Lewis's autobiographical *Main Street* prompted his whole hometown to hate him, sue him, and throw figurative rocks at him until he died, and then they erected monuments in his honor.

After a time, a writer's real life and creative life become entwined very closely, like a vine taking hold of the garden, so that when people ask, "Is this real? Did this really happen?" I am sometimes unable to remember.

---

19 Don't Neglect Research, but Don't Overdo It.

When a writer begins to write, he generally writes off what is called "the top of his head," meaning he writes what he knows the most about, whatever is in his head. Eventually, when he wants to sell his work (excepting the personal essay), he finds he doesn't have enough in his head about, say, raising sugar beets for a profit, to make a fully fleshed-out article. Whether an editor asks him for the article or he writes it on his own, if he wants it to be meaty and impart valid information, he has to go to the library. His own head is not enough. He must do research.

Besides nonfiction articles, stories and novels may require research. Historical dates must be accurate even in a fiction piece. If your setting is Europe in the sixteenth century, you must know who lived then, what they wore, how they spoke, how they traveled, what wars were being fought, etc. Even a very short story must be historically accurate. When I wrote the *Kitty* books I could write from the top of my head for the most part, but did they have nylons then? What year was the last car made before the war? How often did the trains run? A fiction story needs a valid setting. So I found myself doing research because I didn't remember everything about the period that I thought I knew.

Research becomes a pitfall only when it is 1) overdone, or 2) underdone. One happens as frequently as the other. And one is just as bad as the other.

1) Underdone research: You can only get by so long by pretending you know about a subject. No matter how many buzz words you use (jargon to sound knowledgeable, like "constitutional psychopathic inferior" in an article on personalities) or big words ("preprandial libation" in an article on food and drink) you will soon be found out.

Make an outline of your subject and see just what is important for you to know. The *how, what, when, why* things. The things that any reader of your article is going to ask and expect to find, judging from your title. Do not look up any more than you need to know. Keep the reader in mind. Get the information in your notebook or on tape, and come home and pick and choose what is essential.

How will you know if you have done enough research? When you think you have answered all potential questions on the subject, send it to an appropriate market. If the editor writes back that it is shallow, or topical, or superficial, you may not have done enough research. Go back to the library or encyclopedia and garner more data. Well-researched and well-presented material is always in demand. Don't shortchange your reader.

2) Overdone research: It is very easy to fall into the role of the perpetual researcher. Gathering data in a library for six months to write a 300-word article on baby seals is an example of this. Some people love libraries and love research and love gathering facts more than they love writing itself, and by long hours spent in researching they avoid writing (or put it off) for months. The

result is a very low production level. If an editor wants the piece, he or she wants it by deadline. If you want to earn money writing about baby seals and other things, you won't earn much if every piece takes you too long.

On top of the obvious time problem, your writing could become too wordy, too technical, and too long to sell. Everyone is familiar with articles that look intriguing, but when you read them they seem to lack personality or style, and concentrate instead on lists of facts. If an article has too many facts it is boring, even to one who loves the subject. It is an author's style that keeps you reading, that hooks you. If none of the style is allowed to show because the piece reads like a technical handbook, attention can wander.

It is best to present just enough research to grab and hold the reader. If he wants to know more details about the subject, you can refer him to other books on the subject. Or he can go and look it up on his own. It pays to be an adequate researcher, not a perpetual one.

---

20 Don't Write All "I" and "Me" Things. Use the Third Person When You Want to Publish.

When I began writing, I couched everything I wrote in the first person. IIIIII. Always "I" and "me." It was comfortable, it made me honest, and no one told me it was a bad thing to do. It isn't bad, but it isn't always appropriate. I grew so used to it, and settled in, that when the editor of an oil company slick asked me to do a nonfiction article on genealogy, I did it in first person—*My* life, *My* grandmother, *My* experience.

When I proudly sent in my article, he wrote back, said he liked it very much, but would I please change all those "I" and "we" statements to "he," "she," "it," or even "they." In other words, rewrite it in third person. He said most articles are written in the third person, and when he received first person articles, it sounded to him like "a housewife taking her turn at the typewriter!" Today I might have screamed "Discrimination!" but as a beginning writer I was eager to please and had to admit it read more objectively when I'd finished.

Nowadays, under the catch-all of "New Journalism," it is more popular to combine an essay-style first person with fairly objective subject matter, in other words—to write nonfiction in a fiction style. But for a beginning writer, when starting to write for publication, third person still makes a more objective and professional appearance on an editor's desk.

The suggestion I give my students is this: When you begin as a new writer, begin with first person. Write essays, poetry, and most especially journals and diaries, all in first person. "I" did this, "I" did that. It will free you to be more open and honest. Keep that up as long as you need to and are comfortable with it. Then, when you want to write nonfiction for publication, transpose your things into third person. Write articles that way for awhile, submit them that way, and publish them. (The exception is essay writing, which is almost always first person, even for publication.) After you have proved that you can do this and publish, it's time to:

Go back to first person and try an article. Now it won't sound as it did the first time. It will have a more polished feel, a professional appearance. It is like knowing the rules before you break them—beginning in first person, then going to third, and then going back to first, this time with new wisdom, skill, and insight.

If you never do go from first to third, you won't grow, and you'll run the risk of hearing an editor's biting words: It sounds like a housewife taking her turn at the typewriter!

21 Don't Be Afraid to Rewrite.

There is a great temptation, when you finish a piece, to get it right out to an editor. Before you do that, *put it in the icebox*, as the old saying goes. Let it cool. When you read it over in two weeks, the weak spots will jump right out at you, and you can do some revising.

One thing you may notice after the cooling-off period is that whole groups of words can be deleted without being missed. Omit them. Where you digressed, cut. Where you were wordy, cut. Where you used that extra adjective, cut. And where you were redundant, cut.

Read your work with a cold eye, the eye of an objective bystander, the eye of an editor. See if your structure is sturdy. A friend and I used to liken a piece of writing to building a house; once you have the framework up and the foundation built, the rest is easy. You can move furniture around all you like if the house is built.

Look at your pacing and transitions with a cold eye, too. This is no time for emotions to get in the way, no time to hang on to the little story you always loved about Aunt Tillie when you know Aunt Tillie has no business in this story at all. Put the blue pencil through Aunt Tillie. You can use her in another story.

Lastly, check your punctuation and spelling. Even though it is not as important as the idea and the structure, you want to put your best foot forward. You want to send out the best-looking manuscript you can. If you've done all that, you are ready. Instead of the icebox, your manuscript is ready for the mailbox— the place every edited, rewritten manuscript should go!

22 Don't Be Obsessed with Trivial Concerns.

Obsessive trivial concern one: "Will publishers steal my ideas?"

Maybe. Probably not. Most magazines have enough writers and enough material and enough unsolicited manuscripts not to need to steal things. If you are writing something they can use and it is well done, they will be glad to pay for it. Publishers don't usually succeed by preying on freelancers.

There is no guarantee it can't happen, but to spend time brooding over the worry is unproductive. Suppose they do print a story with your idea. Write another article. Change the slant. They would hardly print a "stolen" story just as it is, and ideas are not copyrightable. You may think someone has stolen your idea because you see an article on it the month after you submitted one on the same subject. Chances are they bought that one long before they saw yours. Many articles are written with the same idea. So whether they do, or whether they don't have a similar story, it is not worth the worry. Your things are basically covered by the "Common Law" copyright, and when you sell something it should be to a magazine that is copyrighted. Book publishers will copyright your story in your name when they publish it.

Until then, trust the editors, and remember that even if you think your idea was stolen, it probably wasn't.

Obsessive trivial concern two: "I like my story just as it is; I won't change a word."

An attachment to one's own words to the point of obsession should be brought up here because it is something that I hear so frequently. Clutching his manuscript to his chest, he says, "Unless it will be printed just as it is, I won't let it go." Every comma, every adjective, every qualifier, this writer guards in a personal manner, feeling it is part of his innermost being, his very soul. The creative muse should not be disturbed by something as cold and technical and unartistic as punctuation, grammar, structure, and syntax. These writers enamored of their own words are common, but until they are able to view their work objectively and release it to editorial scrutiny, they are not ready for the world of publication.

Obsessive trivial concern three: Perfect manuscripts. "My manuscript isn't in good enough shape to send out; I made a mistake on page 89 and had to use liquid paper."

Twenty-pound bond with rag content is good to use. New typewriter ribbon is good to use. But if you don't use these, and if you are not an A-1 typist, and if you have to cross out a word or two, an editor will still read and buy the manuscript, *if* you have something to say that that editor wants to hear. Who would pass up a terrific idea, offered in competent writing, on a subject the editor wanted and had not used in the recent past? No doubt the manuscript will have more marks on it before it is finished, blue-pencil editing marks and "omit" marks and "Please add here" marks. Don't lose sleep over that misspelled word on page 4, or that smudge on page 18. Try for perfection, and if you don't make it, send the manuscript anyway. Concentrate on what you are writing. Perfect that. What you have to say is what matters. If your manuscript is pristine white, crisp, and without error, but your article is clichéd and old hat, it will come back to you in the next mail.

In all fairness to those whom I have solicited for opinion on this matter, I must add that although I do not seem to encounter writers who submit sloppy, messy manuscripts, others do. And editors do. So I must note that of course it is not good to type on brown wrapping paper or pink tissue paper, or submit carbon copies or copies with coffee stains and pizza sauce on them. It is not good to single-space a story, or even send computer copies in dot matrix or, God forbid, handwritten copy. But this is the other end of the spectrum, and seems self-evident. My own experience has been with writers who are obsessed with cleanliness and perfection. To those I say: There is a time to stop perfecting the physical appearance and put the manuscript in the mail. Like research, some is a good thing, and too much will keep you from finishing at all.

Obsessive trivial concern four: Waiting for the perfect writing conditions.

Many writers I meet tell me they don't have a quiet place to write. Or they don't have a desk. Or they cannot afford a typewriter. My reply would be go to the library, use the kitchen table, borrow a typewriter, respectively. *Waiting for Perfect Writing Conditions* is like waiting for inspiration or waiting for your children to grow up and leave home—it is just an extension of *procrastination* and can keep you from writing forever.

The light may never be right. Your office may never have a leather-topped desk. The children (some children) may always play with your scotch tape. The dog may always eat your erasers (unless you get rid of the dog). In the history of the greatest authors of the greatest books ever written, almost none of them had ideal working conditions. Most of them were poverty-stricken and were lucky to have a pencil. Yet, with what they had, they eked out some of the strongest prose ever written.

What they had was an overwhelming urge and talent to write, a drive that surpassed all interest in the tools, the accoutrements, the trappings. They wrote because they loved to write by any means at their disposal and in any place that sheltered them from the elements. I am sure some of them wrote with icy fingers. Dostoevski claims he had the worst working conditions of any author alive at the time. Poe was penniless and died in a sewer. Carl Sandburg was born on a corn-husk mattress and his father earned sixteen dollars a month, so when Carl began to write you can be sure the conditions were not aesthetically pleasing or physically luxurious.

The essays and articles I wrote on my card table by hand and typed on an old manual Underwood sold for the same amount of money they would have had they been written in an oak-paneled study. And I could oversee the children and the entire household from my vantage point. It was only when I got an oak desk years later, in fact, that I got writer's block with it. When conditions get too good, there is a real pressure to "write as good" as your conditions are. At my card table, set up hastily every morning after breakfast, I felt spontaneous and prolific and free to concentrate on my words, not on the ring my coffee cup might make on the wood, or the spent batteries in an automatic pencil sharpener.

Virginia Woolf's "room of one's own" is a nice thing to have, but it's not essential. And Faulkner's Rowan Oak estate and the fact that Hemingway built the first swimming pool in Key West do not mean that every author needs luxury to write.

Whether you do or whether you don't have ideal writing conditions, the main thing is not to lose sight of your primary objective: After the conditions are as good as you can make them, the important thing is to write, wherever and however you can.

23 Don't "Want Everyone to Read It!"

It would be nice if what we write could be so universal, could have so much reader-identity, could be so broad without being general, that everyone in the world would want to read it. It sounds good, but it's just not achievable. Writing for everyone is like writing for no one. You need to keep an audience in mind. This is what's meant by the "slant" of writing—for whom are you writing; what do you want them to know?

In fiction (except in genre writing) where you are not writing to "fit" a market, I believe the best person to write for is yourself. I write all of my things for myself, because I am interested, and because I need to say them. Yet, in the very back corner of my mind, out of sight but not quite out of mind, a small *other reader* must be lurking. Somewhere back there I know that I want someone else to read this besides me. Surely I have in mind, in this book, that writers and potential writers will be reading it. Sometimes when I finish a story I just slip into the head of a reader for a moment—or into the head of an editor—and read it through his eyes, a kind of censoring process. So I can't be writing entirely for myself, even though I profess to do so.

It is a common question for juvenile book writers to hear, "What age child did you have in mind when you wrote the book?" Here, very clearly, I cannot tell. "I write all books for me," I say, "and hope that if I like it, some age child will, too." And then I let an editor decide on the age and doctor up the vocabulary until before long I start thinking in that age vocabulary myself.

When I wrote *Near Occasion of Sin*, I was writing an adult book. It sold as a Young Adult. I don't know why, but every editor said, "This is a YA, not an adult." I wrote it for myself, which is a fiction writer's best bet.

Sometimes it's obvious who the reader is. If you write about a new kind of power tool, you have in your mind (besides yourself) a picture of the reader—a carpenter or craftsman, a reader of *Popular Mechanics*. If you write about your dog, you may have other pet owners in mind. If you do a story about a running marathon, you have fellow runners in mind.

My best advice here is to keep your reader in mind and think about what he wants to know. And if you don't know who your reader is, you can't go far wrong in writing for yourself.

24 Don't Listen to Opinion and Criticism from Spouses, Friends, and People on the Street.

If I had to list the single most important reason for my success in publishing, I would say it was because I protected myself from all criticism. Those beginning years, when I loved every word I wrote with passion, I instinctively set up a rule that said, "I'll read my manuscript to no one until it is sold." I didn't want criticism from anyone: family, friends, writers, experts, or nonexperts. Instinct told me it would be destructive to my career. I told myself that the only one I would listen to regarding my manuscripts would be an editor who wanted to buy it. Once it was purchased, I would read it to anyone. Criticism or opinion didn't touch me then—I was professional. My story was sold. It didn't matter what anyone said.

Because protection of my work is so natural to me, I can never understand why students let themselves be so vulnerable. They come to my class saying, before they read their piece, "My husband just loved this," or about a children's story (I hear this one most frequently): "My sister teaches third grade and she read it to her pupils and they just loved it."

Of course they loved it. They love their teacher, and their teacher said, "My sister wrote this story, and it is just wonderful." Of course they respond. Of course they love it. None of that means anything. In the first place, it doesn't really matter what children think of a children's story. That sounds indeed crass, but at the beginning stage it is not a child who must love your story, it is an editor. Very few books are purchased by children. Most books are purchased by librarians and schoolteachers. And a few by parents. If you are writing to publish, you write what an editor wants—the one with the money and power to make your story into a book.

Other students say, "My husband hates this; he says it's no good"—even more damaging to a fragile new writer's ego. And either way, positive or negative, the criticism is probably not valid. Most husbands and friends are not writers and therefore have no criteria. They make personal judgments at best, colored by kinship or friendship, or even anger or jealousy.

So much for criticism from family and friends. Avoid it. But what about criticism from teachers, other writers, and classes? My own opinion is that you will do much better if you stay home and write, and perfect your craft by evolution, by practice (like piano) and by trial and error. I once heard of an author who was besieged by writers wanting to hear him and read for him. After one lecture, he put his hand out for silence and said, "How many of you here want to be writers?" Everyone in the auditorium raised hands. He said, "Then why aren't you home writing, instead of here listening to me?"

In my classes, almost all writers say they are there because they want help. They say they want the truth about their work; they want an objective opinion about how to improve it. Almost all of them—perhaps *all* of them—do not want criticism, no matter how effective. They want praise. That is what they are really there for. Praise. They want someone to say, "That is perfect. It shows great talent. It will sell immediately." Moreover, they want to take it one step further. They want the teacher to say, "It is so good that I will send it off myself, to my own editor. I will sell it for you."

Let us take yet another possibility. Say that the manuscript of this student does need work. Say that the teacher gives very concrete, constructive help, and the writer is not threatened and takes the advice and changes the manuscript. I would say that for every teacher or Reliable Authority the student read to, he would have that many Valid Criticisms, no two alike. I have seen students in search of the Perfect Critique, students who go from class to class for help with the same dog-eared manuscript, and every suggestion they receive may be valid, and every one different. Which one is the most valid? Which one is the Ultimate Criticism? And will a student keep rewriting over and over? I have seen this happen many, many times. I maintain that criticism is most valid from someone who has a vested interest in your work. If you have to shop around, do it with editors.

In my early days at the typewriter I sent manuscripts out over and over again, and received rejection after rejection. But finally I found an editor, one who sensed the glimmer of hope in that hodgepodge of my early work. Editors are not gods. They do not know all the answers. But when you find the right ones they do have something in common with you—they want to improve your work so that it can earn money for both the publisher and you, so that it will be successful for both the publisher and you. You can't beat that combination.

Be willing to work with an editor. Be willing to take his suggestions and at least try them. I am not disqualifying teachers. After all, I am one! But I do see too many students looking for the perfect class and perfect critique when it would profit them more to be home writing. One class, one writer's conference is a learning experience. More than that may evade the real doing. Classes and conferences can also be places to talk about writing instead of writing writing.

Once you do find an editor to take criticism from, expect to make changes in your manuscript. After forty books of my own, I am still in the process of rewriting the last one with my editor. I would be very suspicious of any editor who said, "This is perfect as is. It needs no revision." If that day ever comes, I would probably doubt the editor's ability. When students tell me they want to sell, but they don't want to "change one word," I tell them they want to write for themselves, not the public.

Editors, too, can tell you the *slant* of what they want—it's hard for a teacher or another writer to do that. This book, for example, had a very different slant the first time I wrote it, which means that when I wrote it for *me* it was slanted more generally. The *mistake* slant gave it a more direct theme, better organization, and directed it toward a specific readership.

Editors can also point out your strengths and weaknesses. One editor in my past didn't use essay style (I had been writing and selling essays prolifically), but he asked me to try my first how-to article. I never would have tried how-tos if he had not suggested it. So editors can open up new vistas in writing, suggest you try things you have not done before. I went on to do several articles for his magazine at good pay, better than essay pay. He is the one who suggested I try an article on genealogy—how to trace a family history. I didn't even know my grandmother's maiden name at the time, but I'd read that a writer never says no to an editor and I gave it a try.

I have had editors suggest I turn a poem into a prose piece, and an essay into verse. My editor at Houghton Mifflin reads my novels with an objective eye, removes a chapter here, tells me to add another there, and suggests we move one up front or farther back. And every book is stronger for her opinion. She spots redundancies that I have been too close to see. I might have rewritten a novel completely on the opinion of a friend and never have touched on what it really needed.

Even though I seem adamant about these mistakes, everyone is at a different stage of writing, and sometimes what one person needs badly at one time would not work at all for another. So here, as with any book, a writer has to take what is of value to him at the moment and leave the rest. I don't believe in absolutes. If reading your manuscript to others is the shoe that fits now, wear it.

25 Don't Search for a Talent Scout.

If there is one question I have been asked more than any other (except "Where do you get your ideas?") it is, "Will you tell me if I have any talent?" Many writers seem to be sure that if they only find out for sure that they have talent, their worries will be over. They are afraid of putting in years of work, only to find at the end of the road (or their life) that they were never really writers— that they lacked talent all along.

"If you need someone to tell you, you probably haven't." That is my quote and can apply to a number of things, but one of them is surely talent. When students ask me if they have talent I would like to tell them (but I don't always), 1) that I don't want that responsibility on my shoulders—the making or breaking of a writer. Why should I decide? And 2) I tell them the violin story borrowed from Lawrence Block.

A man once wanted to become a famous violinist. He loved the violin. He worried, though, about whether or not he had talent. He said, "Someday I will play for Mr. Heifetz, the greatest violinist of all, and if he says I have talent, I will pursue a career in music. If not, I'll get a job in a bank." Time went by and eventually he got his wish—he played for the master. Afterwards he waited breathlessly for the response. His whole future hinged on the master's reply.

"Tell me," he said anxiously. "Do I have talent? Do I have the makings of a successful violinist?"

The master shook his head. "You don't have the fire," he told him.

The would-be violinist was a broken man. But he had heard it from the master. He would give up his career in music and go into another field of work. He became a very successful businessman, and many years later, after a concert he went backstage to thank Mr. Heifetz for the words that changed his life. As he shook his hand, he said, "It was because of you that I gave up violin and went into business."

"What did I tell you?" asked the master, frowning.

"You said I did not have the fire."

"Oh," said the master, waving the comment away. "I tell everyone that. Anyone who would come and ask me doesn't have enough belief in himself to succeed."

I *knew* I was a writer; as with criticism, I would never put myself in a position to be told I wasn't. That is the fire—the belief that you will make it no matter what anyone says. If that is not burning inside—that sense of destiny, that desire to succeed, that attainment of a goal at any cost, that *priority*—then all the talent in the world won't help.

There are many people with talent. Not all of them succeed. I used to go so far as to say a person only needs 5 percent talent and 95 percent drive, because I believed drive, the ability to withstand rejection, and perseverance were more important than talent. I don't believe that anymore. But I do believe they are equal. A person does need talent. I see it more every day. If there is not some native ability, some indefinable thing you can't put your finger on, that "flair for words," it would be difficult to succeed. But if, like the violinist, you lack the fire, the talent won't do you any good at all. Lawrence Block, who writes a column on fiction every month for *Writer's Digest*, says many things worth noting, one of them being that he can tell his students if they have talent, but he cannot tell them if they *don't*. He cannot tell them they are not talented, only that their talent is not visible. He also says writing can be learned but it cannot be taught.

I'm not sure what conclusions you can draw from all this information on talent. Perhaps only that talent is very important, but it is not enough. And that if you need to shop around for someone to tell you that you are talented, you may not have the fire.

26 Don't Think an Agent Will Solve All Your Problems.

I've heard lots of beginning writers say, "I wrote a wonderful book. If only I had a good agent, I could sell it." If the book is "wonderful," you can sell it yourself. An agent cannot sell anything that you cannot sell. A direct quote from an agent is, "An agent cannot make anything happen. An agent can only maximize what would happen anyway."

I have sold forty books without an agent. I never had an agent. I play with the idea every once in a while, and the thought entertains me, but in the end I put the idea away. This does not mean that agents are not useful. They are useful in examining contracts, in getting larger advances, in obtaining other rights, like film rights. And of course they have connections and the knowledge of who wants what. If you are ready for an agent, there is a fine list of *bona fide* ones in *Writer's Market*.

But if you think you cannot sell your story without an agent, you are wrong. And even an editor who is well-connected to an agent will not buy anything that he would not buy from you. He won't buy something from an agent unless he likes or wants it. An agent does not make an unsalable piece of work salable.

There are some publishers who say, "Submissions only through an agent," but there are just as many who still read unsolicited manuscripts. Someday, when you have sold enough on your own, you may want or need an agent. The main thing is not to think that an agent will improve your writing, or that you absolutely cannot write or sell without an agent. A hang-up like that is unproductive and self-defeating, and the time wasted trying to find an agent who will take you on is time you could use writing and marketing your own work.

27 Don't Be Taken In by the Get-Rich-Quick Myth. It Takes Ten Years to Become an Overnight Success.

Why is it that everyone thinks writers are rich? The word *writer* gives the man on the street an impression of wealth—eccentricity perhaps as well, but first of all, a lot of money. Turn *writer* to *author*, and he expects you to dress like Barbara Cartland, drive a Mercedes, and live on the Riviera. The truth is, B. Cartland is one of a very few. More writers live in the poverty zone than people in any other profession. Most have to supplement their below-average incomes in ways that are probably detrimental to the creative spirit they hope to nurture.

When a potential writer believes this myth it's dangerous, because he is not facing reality. Earnest writers come to me very frequently asking, "When do you think I should quit my job?" I remind them of their insurance, vacation, health care, dentist, wife, children, mortgage. They wave their hand and say they are willing to "give it up" to get out of the rat race and into the aesthetic, to devote themselves full time to their talent.

Most of those who are ready to give up all are eager to run away *from* something. They are eager to suffer for the muse. And almost all of them, no matter how good they are or how talented, are without contacts in the publishing world. They have no idea of marketing, or assuming the role of one who is self-employed. If they cannot establish themselves in the business before they leave their job, they probably cannot do it afterwards. They may need an agent but can't get one because they have not sold their work.

I have a good friend who began publishing five years ago. She had a very good job, and kept it until this year, when she was selling four books a year, with large advances from a major house. Finally she was earning half as much as her nine-to-five job paid her, so she left the job. Without benefits or vacation, or, more important, any assurance at all that someone would continue to buy four of her manuscripts a year!

Do you sell four books a year? Two magazine articles a month? Hold on to your job then, until you have at least a foot in. Freelancing is precarious to a full-timer, and you may rue the day you said good-bye to your boss.

An author is only as good as his last book, they say. His last *sold* book. Even after selling forty hardcover books and 160 magazine articles, I have no certainty that it will continue—no written contract, no one offering to pay my gas bill, or put food on my table, or buy whatever I might write. Each and every article and book is judged on its own merits. No one will buy it because I have been "successful in the past." I perhaps sound like a pessimist, when actually, there is not a job in the world I would take over my own. It is the best one in the world, for me. But from a realistic point of view, it is not the best job for many.

"How much money do you make?" is the third question I'm most frequently asked. I hold up one of my picture books, which sells for $10.95 (the most recent and most expensive). I say, "The royalty I get on that would be ten percent, which would be a dollar ten for every book that is sold. But I must share that with the illustrator, Lillian Hoban in this case. Or she could say she must share it with *me*. At any rate, I then get only half. She surely did as much work as I did, in illustrating it. We each get five percent. That means for every book that is sold, we each get fifty-five cents! Think of how many books would have to sell to schools, libraries, and bookstores, before a writer could become rich! Some books net me only twenty-five cents, some that have no pictures, one dollar. And no one knows if the book will sell one thousand copies, or ten thousand, or somewhere in between."

Magazine articles pay from $50 to perhaps $500 (if you are well known). But can you sell one or more every single month? And taxes must come out of that, with no employer to pay half of the Social Security. Authors pay twice as much Social Security tax as salaried workers. If you write books, reprint paperback rights may add to your income. So may film rights. And book clubs. Then again, your work may have no sub-right potential at all.

So much for the *get rich* myth. But what about the *quick*? It takes time to write a book or article—maybe months, maybe years. It takes more time to sell it—maybe months, maybe years. After that, it often takes a year or more before the publisher prints it! Then it may take over a year to realize any money from royalties because the advance must be paid back.

Advances can range from $500 for a beginner to over $5,000 for a genre book, such as a Harlequin romance, by an author who is recognized and has a following. But all advances are a sort of loan by the publisher until the books are sold. If your book does not earn more than the advance you received, there *are* no royalties. Royalties are usually paid every six months (unlike paychecks every other Friday in some offices), and of course do not go on forever. After a sort of "peak" period a year after publication, royalties may taper off in the third and fourth year until finally most books go out of print.

So if you like to write, fine. If you *love* to write, better. And if you don't have a large family to support or unpaid bills, the best. But the main thing is, don't begin by falling for the myth that you can *get rich quick*. It simply ain't so.

28 Don't Send a Gothic Novel to *Humpty Dumpty* Magazine. Study Your Markets Before You Submit.

When I began writing, I didn't know that *Writer's Market* existed. I knew about only a handful of magazines, like *McCall's* and *Good Housekeeping* and *Esquire*, and looked in the front of them for the editorial office address. What a short-sighted method, even for a beginner! It must turn editorial hair gray overnight, these inappropriate submissions to publishers. If they are patient at all, they will tell you to "Read the magazine!"

Being a writer does not qualify anyone as a business person. A writer may not like to type, to keep books, to look for markets, to submit manuscripts, and yet this is such an integral part of writing for publication that it cannot be overlooked. Most writers tire of writing for themselves. If they persist in writing they want to move on from their journals to things others will read. Writers write to be read, and when publishing gets into a writer's blood (usually very soon) the writer sometimes finds he knows nothing about marketing. There are many fine books on the subject and so I am only going to hit the gravest mistakes here—not teach procedure. But one of the gravest errors is not reading the magazine or newspaper, or book lists of publishers. It is a waste of postage, of an editor's time, of your own time in selling your story.

If you write gothics, read gothics. If you write articles, read articles. Note where you read them, and what kinds of things are used. Note the slant of the magazine. Is it a family slant? A playboy slant? Does that publisher put out books of fantasy? Does it publish any other books about talking animals? Look in the bookstores and send for their lists. Read *Publishers Weekly* and see what is on whose list. Best of all (but no substitute for reading the magazine) is reading *Writer's Market*, where the requirements are listed clearly along with the editor's name and address. Don't send your gothic to *Humpty Dumpty*. Don't send your love poem to *Business Week*.

Another submissions pitfall is something I find hard to believe, but editors assure me it occurs: handwritten manuscripts and query letters. Handwritten work disqualifies your efforts immediately. It is doubtful (but possible, I suppose) that a work of great merit would be found, written by someone who does not take the trouble to type. Even if it had merit, it would probably be ignored because of its appearance.

I have run into students who want to do something to be noticed by an editor. They want to submit manuscripts on pink paper, or wrapping paper, or use red envelopes of the wrong size. They will of course be noticed, and the negative effect will linger. At the very least, deviating from the norm in any way will announce *not professional*. Type your things on good white bond with rag content and double space them. Keep a carbon of all your work, but don't send carbons to editors. Good, clear photocopies may be sent. Do not type on both sides of the paper! (What is it about writers and paper? A possessive spirit, a holdover from the wartime paper drives?)

If your manuscript is more than five pages, do not fold it. Do not staple it, no matter what the length. Do not bind it. (Paper clips are OK, but can leave marks on the paper.) Use plain white bond No. 10 envelopes, or 9x12 manila envelopes. Don't forget to send return postage. Remember, no one asked you for your manuscript. You are sending it unsolicited, and to expect a publisher to pay postage on the thousands of unasked-for manuscripts he receives would be presumptuous. Do not query by phone unless you know the editor very well. Check up on your manuscript (if you must) by mail.

Do not expect an editor to *tell you what is the matter with your story or article*. His job is to run a magazine and find appropriate material for it; it is not his business to tell you anything except yes or no. If he does say something personal, it may mean that he sees hope in your work, and means to encourage you to send him something else that is more suitable.

Submission suggestions: Think of appropriate markets while your story or book is still fresh in your mind after you have written it. Study *Writer's Market* and other sources, and on the back of your carbon copy, or on small white index cards, list ten of the most appropriate places. Then when it is rejected by one, you need not do the discouraging work of looking for markets again. You need only write the next publisher's address on a fresh envelope and pop it in the mail the same day. Listing markets ahead of time keeps manuscripts off your desk or dining room table and in the mail where they belong. Just put the date that you send it out after the publisher's name, and after that the date that it returns. With ten markets listed, even a friend or relative could mail it out in your absence when you are away.

Don't reassess the story every time it comes back. After trying ten markets (in over a year) reread it and see if you still like it,
and if so, perhaps it needs retyping. Make changes then if need
be, and sit down and list ten more markets that seem appropriate. After trying all of these, you may begin again with the first
one on your list, since there have probably been editorial changes
and policy changes in two years. I have sold many things by sending them to a market where they were rejected previously. One
time the very same editor read the article! (Use your own judgment about mentioning a manuscript's earlier submission. I don't
think it's necessary.)

Always query about longer nonfiction pieces before you send
the whole article or book. Querying will tell you if the magazine
or publisher has just published something similar in the recent
past. It will also tell you the audience. If the editor is interested
he or she will tell you how to slant the article and adjust your
style and content to fit. A query can also give you the word count
that is appropriate. Why write 4,000 words if they can only use
2,000?

When you study the markets, look for trends. In children's
books, for example, there has been an overdose the last few
years of single-parent books, divorce books, death-of-grandpar-
ents books, and racial minority books. When my book *My Daddy
Lost His Job Today* didn't sell for several years, I changed it to
My Mother Lost Her Job Today, in time for the role-reversal
trend, and sold it.

So put your best foot forward, and avoid the submission error.
It will make the difference between a sale and a rejection.

29 Don't Give Up!

In the end, the difference between a published writer and an unpublished one comes down to one thing: The unpublished writer
gave up, and the published writer didn't.

I was gathering old manuscripts and correspondence together yesterday at the request of a university library (which keeps all of my old notes, paper napkins with cryptic jottings, and even my misplaced grocery list in climate-controlled vaults) and I glanced at one of the carbons on which I had listed the places that manuscript had been peddled. They were scribbled on the margins, on the back, even right on top of the text when room had run out. Long-gone dates jumped out at me, and I began to count how many places the manuscript had been before it sold and ended up in a university collection. Just the one I looked at by chance (to say nothing of the other ten) had been to *thirty-four* publishers, rejected, and returned!

Have you sent your stories to thirty-four places? I thought not. No one I talk to does. Writers instead send something out, and if it is returned they take it as a personal insult, or worse yet, they believe it has no worth and they file it. I am sure, in going through the classics, you will find examples of multiple rejections, with the authors sometimes even resorting to self-publishing. But the publishers were wrong, the author was right, and the book, lasting through centuries, proved it so.

Writers tend to think that there is some Ultimate Criterion, some sort of arrival point they need to attain (always elusive), and then they will sell. They often believe that every editor behind every desk in every publishing company holds some secret to the Perfect Book (or article or essay or poem) and it is up to the writer to detect this secret.

Writer, there *is no secret*. There is no objective criterion. There are only Persons behind those desks, who sigh at the influx of mail with handwritten manuscripts and no self-addressed stamped envelopes, and writers who stumble into the pitfalls I've mentioned. But they are willing to pay money for and publish whatever good comes across their desks, and the "good" is something they like. If you avoid most of these mistakes, if you write with talent and skill, the rest is dependent on an editorial whim. This is not a great truth, or secret. It is up to you simply (by trial and error) to find that person who thinks about life in the same way you do, who has not published something on the same subject recently, who likes your style, who says, "I felt that way once! I think I'll buy this."

Buying your work is a subjective decision for editors. They have their own criteria, their own backgrounds of experience, their own foibles and pet peeves. It is like a match game—you keep submitting until you match. Editor one says, "Good theme, original, right length, but I hate cats, so I won't buy." Editor two says, "I love cats, it's original, good theme, but it is way too long, so I can't use it." Editor three may say, "Good theme, right length, original, and I love cats. I'll buy it."

You have to get all of your assets together with someone else. And you must keep trying until you do.

It sounds as if I am saying that all manuscripts could sell somewhere, and I can hear editors groan. Well, I think most of them would, if a writer marketed long enough. I am assuming that you are satisfied with your work—that you have done your best, that you have some talent and skill, that you have edited and tightened your work, and that you have studied the markets. If so, and if you believe in a piece of writing and like it, someone else out there will too. But many writers never find out. They give up long before that point.

When I tried my first "concept" book, after publishing five fantasy books with Crown, my publisher didn't want it. I thought of putting it away and forgetting it, but then realized that if I didn't try new things and expand my horizons, I would not grow. I sent it to many other publishers. No one seemed to want it. I read it over, still loved it, knew it had a good plot and a good resolution to the problem, retyped it, and sent it out again. At last, on the twenty-seventh rejection, I found an editor who loved it! She published it, and it is still in print, still selling well. It is called *My Mom Hates Me in January*, published by Albert Whitman. And I have published books with them ever since.

How many times have you sent something out twenty-seven times? There is no cut-off point where you are no longer rejected. No matter how many books I sell, I wonder about the next one. Each one has to communicate with editors all over again. It has to carry its own reputation, not mine. Even my own editor at Houghton Mifflin said in one of her letters, "I don't envy you, having to live by your wits. If it was me, I couldn't write anything funny. I'd be writing Greek tragedy."

When you do find the one who wants your things, be open to revision. When I was beginning, I wrote poetry—very short, some only four lines. I had no idea that four lines would need revision. When I found an editor who wrote on my rejections, "Not right, but try us again," and, "I like this, except for. . ." I decided to take the suggestions she gave and send it back to her. The first poem that she actually bought (for *three dollars!*) went through three more revisions. It went back and forth in the mail until the meter and wording were just right. I can't remember the poem, but I remember working harder for that three dollars than I did later for three thousand. Because I did rewrite it, she bought many other poems from me and was very supportive in my early career. Don't turn down offers to revise. Pay attention to whatever is written on those rejection slips. Fix them up and get them out again.

Watch for places where you think your things will fit. I read a small newspaper in Wisconsin for years, enjoying the column-type reports they did about family foibles. I thought (as you must have also) "I could write something like this." And eventually I thought, "I could write something *better* than this." So I decided to try. I wrote something about my family, one of the many escapades that go on in every home, and sent it off to the editor whose name was listed on the masthead. He rejected it, but wrote an encouraging note. I kept on, and finally sold him an essay. After that I wrote about everything as it happened around me, about haircuts, and Jamie wanting to be a bishop, and tennis rackets, and first days of school, and shopping with teenagers. He bought some, rejected some, but before long he bought more than he returned.

So even if you study all the pitfalls in this book and make sure you avoid them, none of it will matter if you fail to observe this: *Don't give up!*

A Few Last Words

Because I never like to say good-bye, I continue. I feel there should be some sort of closure, some sort of wrap-up. In my lectures I always have a question-and-answer session so that no one will go away and not find out what he came for. Questions also remind me of all those things I wanted to say and forgot. So, what do you want to know that I didn't tell you? Yes, the lady in the back row there . . .

"Do you draw the pictures for your books? I want to write a picture book, but I need pictures to show what I mean."

If your picture book cannot stand on its own, it may not be strong enough for a book. The story should be a unit on its own (once you leave the preschool crowd) and the illustrations should enhance it, but not explain it. If you are not an artist it is best to put your effort into writing a strong story, and let the publisher find a suitable illustrator in his stable of artists (who live in the east and can come into the office with their work). This is not to say you never can illustrate your own books when you live in other places. But if you are not primarily an artist, just concentrate on the text.

Authors tell me that "the illustrator won't know how I think it should look," and the reply is that he had better know how it should look. If you have not managed to convey this in your writing, you'd better try again. A wise editor once told me, "Artists don't tell you how to write, why should you tell them how to draw?" An artist should be at least as creative as a writer. And a good one puts "surprises" into the book; he or she does not just illustrate the words that are in it. In my book *Two Good Friends*, Bear wears elaborately monogrammed clothes and has a Big Bear clock (instead of Big Ben) and a water pitcher with a dancing bear ballerina on it, none of which were in my text. Not all good artists can illustrate books—they must have a feeling for the character that a writer has. An editor should know who is suitable for a certain type of book. But if you want to write a picture book, concentrate on the words, not the pictures.

When I visit schools, a small child will always say, "Do you draw the pictures?" I say no.

Then another says, "Is it hard to sew the covers on?" I admit I don't sew the covers on.

"Is it hard to write all those words so many times in so many books?" I have to say that I only type the words once, and the printer makes the books. By this time I am in total disgrace, and the children are all wondering what in the world an author *does* do.

Any more questions? Yes, the lady in the pink hat . . . .

"Are writers born, or can they learn to be writers? Do you think your children inherited your talent?"

I believe the only inherited things are the shapes of noses and the color of eyes and hair and skin. I think a child's personality is a sum total of how his environment hits him. If children see a mother or father mopping floors, they will mop floors. If they see them reading or writing or digging ditches, they will read or write or dig ditches. I remember being very surprised, when I started school, to find that other fathers did not work at the telephone company, and that not all children took their shoes off on the back porch before they entered the house. Children imitate, and for a long while believe there is only one way to do things—like their parents.

If my children had been adopted by someone else at birth they probably would not write, but would do whatever those parents did. But this is not always a direct imitation. No environment strikes two children in the family the same; they are different people and perceive stimuli differently.

I think my children probably wrote because they saw me writing and believed that was what people did. As they grew up, I was often in my room writing, or reading, and they went to their rooms and wrote at a very young age. Then they began to send things out to publishers because I suggested it. I did not begin to write until I was thirty-nine years old. Before that I did what I saw my parents do—grow up and go to school and get a job. At thirty-nine I deviated from my environmentally conditioned behavior, taking the risk that I'd be without support.

Today, reading my father's letters of the 1920s, I realize that he was a writer too, a writer who never pursued writing. In retrospect also, I realize he was a great help with my school assignments, and everything I remember him writing showed talent and skill. Not all talent is fulfilled.

I believe people who want their children to be "creative" must be creative themselves. You can't "teach" creativity, you can only exemplify it. Creative children have creative parents (or guardians) whether the latter think themselves creative or not. Creativity can be silent, lurking in dark corners of the imagination, and can exhibit itself by mending a broken pipe in the cellar as well as painting a picture.

If I had insisted that my children get into writing, I don't think they would have pursued it. Parents have to leave room for discovery and then encourage the result. My daughter was keeping huge journals, when I suggested she try a book. My other daughter was already writing funny essays when I suggested they fit *Seventeen*'s format. I could be wrong, and talent may be inherited, but I'll vote for environment.

"Do you think I should self-publish my book if no one wants it?"

No. Although publishers have mixed criteria for what they buy, subjective to be sure, subsidy (or "vanity") publishers have almost no criteria. You pay to have your books printed and then you take them home, where you store them in the attic and basement, except for the few you give to friends, *gratis*. And there they stay because you have no marketer or advertiser or distributor. Bookstores won't take them, magazines won't review them, and unless you want to stand on the corner and peddle them, you can't sell them.

Self-publishing (as opposed to vanity publishing) *can* be a good idea if you have enough money and are willing to work hard to market your book. If you want your family history in print for your grandchildren, you can pay to have it printed. If you write local things (such as where the best restaurants and thrift shops and nightclubs are in your area) you can have it printed yourself and distribute it locally. But even these may have rough sledding. You are probably better off finding a publisher who will take a chance on your book and pay the expenses, because if he puts up the money to print the book, he has a vested interest in its distribution and sales. In general, if an editor doesn't think your book or piece will sell, it may mean that selling it yourself would be even more difficult, if not impossible.

All right, one more question—yes, you in the very back row. . . .

"If we avoid all of the mistakes in this book, can you guarantee publication?"

I guess, like all other things in life, there are no guarantees. There are no absolutes when you are dealing with human beings. And publishers and editors are human beings. There is no predicting what people will do. When I swear an editor likes pink, she chooses blue instead. I can only say that if you avoid the mistakes you will have a very good, much better, and even a likely chance of selling. You also must have the Givens: some talent and skill and drive. You have to be a competent writer, and actually have something completed and on paper, before you can avoid the pitfalls.

And I will turn your statement around (I love reversals!) and say that if you *don't* avoid these errors, you won't have much of a chance at all. So there is nothing to lose and everything to gain.

Since our time has run out now (I see the editor pointing to the clock), I suppose I must close. I always hate to go, to take my leave, and therefore hang around places long after the last guest has left. It is the same with ending a book. Did I say enough? Did I say too much? I'll know when I see your name in print!

Index

research for, 43-45
sources for, 15-16
Note making, 16

O

Office people as subjects, 16
Originality
in avoiding clichés, 25-27
in recognizing relationships, 22
Outlining the story, 31-33, 44

P

Perfectionism, 9, 10, 48
Picture books, 12-14, 21, 58, 66
Platitudes, 25-26
Priority setting. *See* Writing priority
Problem and resolution, 15
Procrastination
and commitment, 1
and distractions, 1-3
by overresearching, 44
and priority setting, 1-3
and risk taking, 42-43
by talking writing, 8, 52-53
and warm-up exercises, 4
and writing conditions, 49-50
Publishers Weekly, 60
Publishing, 14, 60-65
Punctuation
checking before submitting, 47
overuse of, 28-29

Q

Qualifiers, 26-27
Queries, 62
Quotation marks, 20

R

Reading
to market, 60
to write, 35-36
Rejections, 62-65
Research, 43-45
Resubmissions, 62-65
Revisions, 64-65

Rewriting, 46-47
with editors, 53-54
refraining from, 16-17
to update, 26
Risk taking, 42-43
Role-playing exercises, 6
Royalties, 58-59

S

Seasonal writing, 4
Self-expression
vs. communication, 34-35
and opinion, 37-39
Self-publishing, 63, 68
Sensory perceptions, 4-5, 17-19
Sermonizing, 18, 37-39
Setting limits. *See also* Discipline
for subject choice, 11
for subjects per story, 10
Simile, 22-23
Slang, 27
Slant of writing, 50-51, 54, 60, 62
Sniffing as inspiration exercise, 5
Source material
childhood memories, 4, 14
conversations, 11-12, 16
friends and relatives, 5, 15-16
looking and listening for, 11-16
magazines, 4
newspapers, 15
for nonfiction, 15-16
television programs, 15
Specifics in writing, 5, 17-19
Stolen ideas, 47-48
Story-telling quality, 10

T

Talent
assessment of, 55-56
heredity or environment? 67-68
and skill, ix
Talking vs. writing, 7-8
Theme
identifying, 29
and interpretation, 30
outlining of, 31-33
and subtlety, 37
Third person, 45-46

About the Author

Judy Delton began writing in 1971. Since then she has published forty books (everything from children's picture books to adult novels) with major publishers and more than 160 articles in periodicals ranging from the *Wall Street Journal* to *Humpty Dumpty*. In 1974, her book *Two Good Friends* was on the American Library Association's list of notable books and in 1977, as a result of her six years of teaching writing for publication at area colleges, she was voted Outstanding Teacher of the Year at Metropolitan State University in Minneapolis. She continues her active writing career and is a frequent lecturer on writing at conferences and seminars throughout the country.

Other Books of Interest

Computer Books

The Complete Guide to Writing Software User Manuals, by Brad M. McGehee (paper) $14.95

The Photographer's Computer Handbook, by B. Nadine Orabona (paper) $14.95

General Writing Books

Beginning Writer's Answer Book, edited by Polking and Bloss $14.95

Getting the Words Right: How to Revise, Edit and Rewrite, by Theodore A. Rees Cheney $13.95

How to Become a Bestselling Author, by Stan Corwin $14.95

How to Get Started in Writing, by Peggy Teeters $10.95

How to Write a Book Proposal, by Michael Larsen $9.95

How to Write While You Sleep, by Elizabeth Ross $12.95

If I Can Write, You Can Write, by Charlie Shedd $12.95

International Writers' & Artists' Yearbook (paper) $12.95

Law & the Writer, edited by Polking & Meranus (paper) $10.95

Knowing Where to Look: The Ultimate Guide to Research, by Lois Horowitz $16.95

Make Every Word Count, by Gary Provost (paper) $7.95

Pinckert's Practical Grammar, by Robert C. Pinckert $12.95

Teach Yourself to Write, by Evelyn Stenbock (paper) $9.95

The 29 Most Common Writing Mistakes & How to Avoid Them, by Judy Delton $9.95

Writer's Block & How to Use It, by Victoria Nelson $12.95

Writer's Encyclopedia, edited by Kirk Polking $19.95

Writer's Guide to Research, by Lois Horowitz $9.95

Writer's Market, edited by Paula Deimling $19.95

Writer's Resource Guide, edited by Bernadine Clark $16.95

Writing for the Joy of It, by Leonard Knott $11.95

Writing From the Inside Out, by Charlotte Edwards (paper) $9.95

Magazine/News Writing

Basic Magazine Writing, by Barbara Kevles $15.95

Complete Guide to Writing Nonfiction, by the American Society of Journalists & Authors $24.95

How to Write & Sell the 8 Easiest Article Types, by Helene Schellenberg Barnhart $14.95

Newsthinking: The Secret of Great Newswriting, by Bob Baker $11.95

Write On Target, by Connie Emerson $12.95

Writing Nonfiction that Sells, by Samm Sinclair Baker $14.95

Fiction Writing

Creating Short Fiction, by Damon Knight (paper) $8.95

Fiction Is Folks: How to Create Unforgettable Characters, by Robert Newton Peck $11.95

Fiction Writer's Help Book, by Maxine Rock $12.95

Fiction Writer's Market, edited by Jean Fredette $18.95

Handbook of Short Story Writing, by Dickson and Smythe (paper) $7.95

How to Write Best-Selling Fiction, by Dean R. Koontz $13.95

How to Write & Sell Your First Novel, by Oscar Collier with Frances Spatz Leighton $14.95

How to Write Short Stories that Sell, by Louise Boggess (paper) $7.95

One Way to Write Your Novel, by Dick Perry (paper) $6.95

Storycrafting, by Paul Darcy Boles $14.95

Writing Romance Fiction—For Love And Money, by Helene Schellenberg Barnhart $14.95

Writing the Novel: From Plot to Print, by Lawrence Block (paper) $8.95

Special Interest Writing Books

The Children's Picture Book: How to Write It, How to Sell It, by Ellen E. M. Roberts $17.95

Complete Book of Scriptwriting, by J. Michael Straczynski $14.95

The Craft of Comedy Writing, by Sol Saks $14.95

The Craft of Lyric Writing, by Sheila Davis $17.95

Guide to Greeting Card Writing, edited by Larry Sandman (paper) $7.95

How to Make Money Writing Fillers, by Connie Emerson (paper) $8.95

How to Write a Cookbook and Get It Published, by Sara Pitzer $15.95

How to Write a Play, by Raymond Hull $13.95

How to Write and Sell Your Personal Experiences, by Lois Duncan $10.95

How to Write and Sell (Your Sense of) Humor, by Gene Perret $12.95

How to Write "How-To" Books and Articles, by Raymond Hull (paper) $8.95

How to Write the Story of Your Life, by Frank P. Thomas $12.95

Mystery Writer's Handbook, by The Mystery Writers of America (paper) $8.95

On Being a Poet, by Judson Jerome $14.95

The Poet's Handbook, by Judson Jerome (paper) $8.95

Poet's Market, by Judson Jerome $16.95

Programmer's Market, edited by Brad McGehee (paper) $16.95

Sell Copy, by Webster Kuswa $11.95

Successful Outdoor Writing, by Jack Samson $11.95

Travel Writer's Handbook, by Louise Zobel (paper) $9.95

TV Scriptwriter's Handbook, by Alfred Brenner (paper) $9.95

Writing After 50, by Leonard L. Knott $12.95

Writing and Selling Science Fiction, by Science Fiction Writers of America (paper) $7.95

Writing for Children & Teenagers, by Lee Wyndham (paper) $9.95

Writing for Regional Publications, by Brian Vachon $11.95

Writing for the Soaps, by Jean Rouverol $14.95

Writing to Inspire, by Gentz, Roddy, et al $14.95

The Writing Business

Complete Guide to Self-Publishing, by Tom & Marilyn Ross $19.95

Complete Handbook for Freelance Writers, by Kay Cassill $14.95

Editing for Print, by Geoffrey Rogers $14.95

Freelance Jobs for Writers, edited by Kirk Polking (paper) $7.95

How to Be a Successful Housewife/Writer, by Elaine Fantle Shimberg $10.95

How to Get Your Book Published, by Herbert W. Bell $15.95

How to Understand and Negotiate a Book Contract or Magazine Agreement, by Richard Balkin $11.95

How You Can Make $20,000 a Year Writing, by Nancy Hanson (paper) $6.95

Literary Agents: How to Get & Work with the Right One for You, by Michael Larsen $9.95

The Writer's Survival Guide: How to Cope with Rejection, Success and 99 Other Hang-Ups of the Writing Life, by Jean and Veryl Rosenbaum $12.95

To order directly from the publisher, include $2.00 postage and handling for 1 book and 50¢ for each additional book. Allow 30 days for delivery.

Writer's Digest Books, Department B
9933 Alliance Road, Cincinnati OH 45242
Prices subject to change without notice.